3 X BETTER

notionpress.com

3 ✕ BETTER

Ovié

notionpress.com

Notion Press

5 Muthu Kalathy Street, Triplicane,

Chennai - 600 005

First Published by Notion Press 2014

ISBN: 978-93-84049-66-9

Dedicated to The Beatles, whose diehard fan I will always be

ACKNOWLEDGEMENTS

First off, I would like to thank my lovely mother for her never-ending support and words of inspiration. She provided me with plenty of confidence and motivated me to finish this project. There were times when I thought I should just give up, but she encouraged me to go ahead. Her 'you-can-do-it's and 'go-for-it's really kept me moving. Also, she reviewed my book and offered constructive criticism and helpful suggestions. I shall always be grateful to her for that. Mother, I love you and respect you.

Next comes my amazing father, who was always there to motivate me, to push me on and to tell me to stop lazing around and to get to work. Father, you rock!!!

Third of all, I say a big 'Thank-you' to my little brother, Aditya, who was always around for a good laugh.

Fourthly, I offer loads of thanks to Miss Rao, who is as wonderful a reviewer as she is a Maths teacher. She helped me loads. Stay cool, Miss!

Fifth of the deal, I am eternally grateful to my friends, who helped me turn a spark of an idea into a full-out flame and were my primary inspiration. I owe everything to you folks.

Sixthly, I thank my absolutely fantabulous publishers for making this book available to the world.

Next in line comes Bill Gates, on whose resourceful MS Word software I typed my whole book out.

And last, but definitely not the least, I thank you, reader, for taking the time to read this. I really appreciate it and I hope you like my book.

May the adventure begin...

- Ovié

Contents

Prologue

"Not without you, mate."

His face was clammy and sweaty, eyes wide and pleading with us. I could see a small tear threatening to fall off the rim of his right eye. "Please," he gasped. "Please do this for me."

"I've made myself very clear."

Will turned to him angrily and said, "Why don't you stop being such an arse and listen to us? We haven't much time; in fact, we haven't almost any time left. Just listen to us, will you?"

"I won't let you two do anything of the sort."

"Face it, chum. There are two of us and you're only one sodding person who's stupidly trying to be a hero. We can easily beat you in an argument."

Martin looked up at the sky. Planes shot across it, dropping grenades and other explosives as they shot across the cerulean sky.

Will said, "There is no use searching for another shelter now. We don't even know where another one will be. Plus, the raid has begun. If we're going to die anyway, let's do so like men."

Martin finally agreed, "We live together or we die together. Nothing else is acceptable."

I allowed myself a weak smile and spoke, "Now, let's face this bloody thing."

We just stood there, smiles on our faces, eyes shining and arms around each other, waiting for death; we were sure it would come soon.

Introduction

Good day, reader. My name is Lew; at least, that's what my friends call me. My full name [I'm not saying I like it very much] is Lord Lewis Edward Candling. My father is one of the richest men in England and I'm his unfortunate heir. Now you must be asking the question-*why in the world is this lad saying that he is unfortunate when his father is affluent and he is his heir?*

The answer to that very question is that my father hates me. He does not want anything to do with me. He has made my life a living hell. Naturally, I get angry sometimes. Once, to punish him, I soaked all his clothes in white-wash. But my actions were justified, right? Right?

Oh...let us forget about that episode! Let me tell you more about myself. I have stormy grey eyes and chocolate-coloured wavy hair. By the way, I look exactly like *him*. Well, I admit to the fact that I got a bit hopeful when I read an advertisement in The London Daily about facial surgeries. I have asked my mother many times for permission to do it, but every time I requested her assent, she just smiled and asked me to accept my looks. And, I'll rather jump off a cliff than ask Candling for permission. Coming to my complexion, it is 'touched by tan'. My height is five feet ten inches, which is good [if not excellent ;)] for a boy of my age, that is, sixteen, but of course Lord Eggplant Crumbling thinks I'm stunted. So, in a nutshell, I look exactly like my father. I hate my looks and can't wait to come of age, so that I finally can get that damn surgery done.

I am in love with music. I really like to sing and strum my guitar. Sometimes, I make up my own lyrics and write my own songs. I want to become a musician when I grow up, but I dare not voice my dreams to my father. I'm sure he'll first whip the Nick out of me and then say that if I don't join the army like he did, he will personally incinerate me. I mean, really, *who* has such a pain in the neck for a father? I hope you do not, reader.

I have just passed my Certificate Examination with distinction from Brooklyn High School. I have gotten a place at Westminster College, where I shall be for two years, and Candling is forcing me to go there. He wants me to get my Bachelors' Degree and then sign up for the army. But, you know what I want to do, don't you? If you are interested in knowing anything about my academic life... well, I am pretty good at English and Math. I get good grades in all the other subjects if I work hard enough. And just so you know, I stood fourth in my form in the C.E.

But Edward Candling the Great [I hope you noticed the sarcasm] says that I have to improve. To be completely honest, I have no idea which cloud he fell from. I just hope he returns to the clouds just as fast, so that there can be some peace on earth.

Also, he expects me to behave like a 'gentleman'. Why, a few days ago, he made me dress up for dinner in one of his *tuxedos* and did his nut when my nose touched the rim of the glass I was sipping water from.

Once, when I was an innocent five year old, he dragged me to get my Barnet chopped in the army style. Even at that tender age, I was highly humiliated by the haircut. My hair was shorn just very slightly shorter than the stubble on Edward Candling's apish face. The next day, when I went to school, my friends teased me horribly. I came back home crying that day, and declined to step within a mile of my school before my hair grew to its normal length again. I refused as vehemently as possible and was as adamant as a bobby soxer, but I was dragged, kicking and screaming, to school.

Finally, my hair became their original length. But again, my father dragged me and had them cut. This went on until I turned eleven. After that, I feigned illness every time he suggested taking me out for a cut. Eventually, he saw right through my act [I'm no good actor] and made to pull me to the private salon, when my good old grandfather [I owe him my life] intervened and asked his son to leave me alone.

You should have seen the way Candling was fuming at him. If you ask me, I think every lad has problems with his father. When I asked Grandpa Hargreaves about it, he said, "You have no idea how your father was." He refused to tell me a single dicky-bird more. After Grandpa Hargreaves left, Father tried to subject me to the numerous tortures of a haircut once more, but I threatened to write to Grandpa and tell him everything. So, to my great glee, Candling gave in, mumbling something that sounded like 'bloody blackmailer'.

Allow me to tell you something about my mother now. She is, of course, according to me, the most beautiful woman on the planet. She has long red hair and amber-coloured eyes. Her complexion is really fair. She looks like one of those princesses from fairy-tales. But, the catch is that in fairy-tales, the princess always marries a handsome prince. And believe me; my old man, he is a total void coupon.

I am now going to tell you a few things about that Billy-goat who calls himself my father. I've already told you what he looks like, but let me give you some accurate details. Just picture me in your mind's eye. Then, make me a few inches taller, tan me highly, give me a muscular frame, add slight stubble to my cheeks, fleck my hair with white here and there and comb it down very neatly. Hey presto! You get Lord Eerily Crippling. He is a retired Colonel from the army-he fought in the Great War, you see. I have also heard that there is a chance that another war may start soon. I don't know why people are so obsessed with fighting each other. But if they all are like my air-headed male designated one, I think it is fine for them to do so for the instinct is inborn within them.

Now, you must be thinking that as I am the son of a filthy rich person, I must be really famous and all that rot. The truth is that I am not an attention-seeking git unlike someone I know. I like to keep a low profile and stay home most of the time. Whenever we have to leave the house to go out somewhere, I just, you know, try not to get noticed too much. And anyway, I do not want to become famous because of something *he* did.

Returning to Colonel Extra Corrosive, he is always giving me long lectures about how I should shed my 'childish, irresponsible ways' and start 'acting like a man'. He wants me to join the army and fight just like he did. But I want to make my dreams come true. I want to become a musician. It has been my heart's desire for many, many years now. My mother is quite fine with me doing whatever I want. But the reason for my miserable home-life is that Lord Cropping wants me to fight in the war and 'die a hero', because apparently, 'man dies but glory lives'.

I, of course, treat the whole thing like absolute tosh, which it is. And I'm sure that if I give vent to my feelings, my rear will never be the same again. But then again, I would love to voice my thoughts. If he wasn't there in my life, I would have been on cloud nine forever. But, I have a cruel, heartless person for a father who mistreats me. But, on a more positive note, I have a feeling that I am going to escape his clutches soon.

Chapter 1
INTO THE WORLD

"…Glory like no other. It is a noble profession and you get to die a heroic death. The army is the perfect place for men. Who would want a better job?"

'*Me!*' I thought. I was getting exasperated of my father's lecture which had gone on for about an hour. I was sitting in front of him with an 'I'm-clearly-not-interested-why-can't-you-see-that' expression on my face. I just wanted to get out of my father's sight and get back to spending time with my most prized possession-my guitar.

But unfortunately for me, I was stuck in a room with an old goat telling me what to do with my life. I had a feeling that I wouldn't be able to get out of the room for at least another hour. It was not an ideal start to my after-examination break that Brooklyn High School generously provided to Certificate students.

"I think you should really join the army and make me proud. You are a pampered brat with no values, no talents and no idea of how harsh the world is. You live in your own 'happy-go-lucky' bubble. The army will prick it and drill some sense into that empty head of yours."

I felt hot anger surge through my body. How could he say that I was no good at anything? I had done well in my examinations. It was true that I could not paint very well, but I covered up for it by being outstanding at music. My mother was always proud of me. So why couldn't Colonel Endless Cruelty just be happy with the son he had rather than the 'picture-perfect' son he wanted? I scowled and glared at the man sitting in front of me.

"You will become a much better individual. You will have your corners rubbed out and your character built well. As I always say, man dies but glory lives. So, I am putting you into boarding school."

He then stopped and looked at me as if he expected me to say something. My mouth was so wide open that our oven could have fit inside it without any sort of problems. I couldn't, and didn't want to, process what he had just told me.

"You can't. You won't...will you?"

He nodded grimly and said, "Boarding school will help you grow up. You are just a weak little wimp right now. Three hard years of hostel will do you good."

I was both surprised and angry. I was surprised because he was actually going to send me to boarding school. And I was angry because he had called me a wimp. So, all I could do was stare open-mouthed at the man in front of me.

After a few minutes, I stood up, cleared my throat and began, "Listen to me, Father. I know that you want me to join the army and fight for Mother England, but that is not the first career choice on *my* list. I want to, from the very bottom of my heart, become a singer and a musician."

Needless to say but I will - he went completely ballistic. "My son, MY SON, wants to become a musician! Do you know, Candling, where you will leave our family's reputation if you do so? What will happen to us? Forget us, what will happen to *you*? Take back your words right now or I will make you do so. You may think that it is an exciting life to become a singer, but let me tell you one thing. You will die in poverty. You will have wasted your life."

All this while, I was simply standing with my arms crossed. I had made up my mind. I spoke calmly, "I've made my decision. I've chosen my future. I may die in poverty, but I will be happy. I'd much rather die happily in poverty than die unhappily surrounded by piles and piles of wealth. Please allow me to become a singer, Father."

His hands were clenched tightly by his sides. Fire was blazing in his eyes. I could tell that he was using up all of his self-control to refrain from hitting me. I did not even turn a hair. It was time for me to tell him what exactly I thought of him and his army.

He finally sputtered, "You are no son of mine." He turned on his heel and started walking towards the door. I muttered something under my breath. He immediately turned and spoke, "Did you say something?"

"Yes," I mumbled.

"Louder!"

"Yes!"

"What did you say?"

"I simply said that I was glad that you said that, because you are no father of mine either. Colonel Candling, you *hate* me. You have never treated me like a son. You have instead treated me like your enemy in war. I am tired of all this. I do not wish to be tortured anymore. I am leaving."

He stood stock-still, unable to believe his ears. He had probably not expected me to wish to leave. He stuttered, "L-l-look, son..." I held up my hand, asking him to stop. I said coolly, "You yourself said, a few moments ago, that I was no son of yours. Forgiven me so soon, Colonel?"

I turned and stormed out of the room. It was the first time I had spoken up to him like that. I figured that was why he was so surprised. I heard fast footsteps behind me. I quickened my pace. I entered my room and brought out a trunk. I pulled the doors of my closet open. My father entered the room.

He said, "Son, I spoke too soon. I do not mean everything I say. The words were out of my mouth before

I had a chance to think. Please do not do so." I gave him an intense shut-up-or-I-swear-I-will-blast-you glare. I said dangerously, "I know why you want to keep me here. You want me to stay in this filthy hole because you just want someone to torment. I think I have held that position for quite a long time. It has been sixteen years."

"You don't understand, Lewis. I just wanted, and still want, to stop you from getting spoilt."

I looked daggers at him and said, "My decision, *Candling*, is final." I felt so angry that if someone would have kept a pot of water on my head, it would have started boiling. I could not think rationally. My senses had most certainly gone for vacation. My body had allowed my emotions to take over.

I stepped up to my father and said, "My decision is not going to change, so don't even think of trying to make me stay. I went over, took my guitar [it was in its case, don't worry] and slung it over my shoulder I, as I later realised, forgot to take along the notebook in which I used to write songs. I went back to him and spoke in my most venomous voice, "I am leaving." With that, I pushed him aside with my heavy trunk and ran for the door. I could hear him following me. I increased my speed and sprinted down to one of the many side-doors of Candling Manor.

At that moment, a door in the corridor opened and my mother stepped out. However, I was going a bit too fast and I banged into her. She looked at me with her amber eyes full of surprise and curiosity. Due to this little collision, Edward Candling had caught up with me. He gripped my arm tightly.

My mother asked, "What is going on, Colonel, Lewis? What happened?"

Oh, and did I mention, he forces her to call him 'Colonel'. Sometimes I think she should just go away for a vacation and never come back. And of course, she should take me with her.

Candling, using his special accept-my-overlordship-or-I-will-skin-you-alive-and-feed-you-to-the-coyotes-when-I-next-go-hunting voice, said, "Our son, Virginia, wants to become a *musician*! I tried to knock some sense into him, but he insists on taking up that abominable profession. He took it into his useless brain to run away, but now I have him."

A strong wave of fury swept through my body again. When I was running away, he had been kind and nice to me. Now when he had me in his grasp, he was back to being devilish to me. Not that I could expect any help from Mother; she always cowers when he uses that voice of his. But, I was in for a surprise.

"Leave him." My mother's hands were clenched into tight fists and on her hips. Her eyes were blazing. I had never seen her stand up to Candling like that. I felt a rush of pride towards her.

"Excuse me?!" Candling was clearly taken aback. I suddenly felt happy. I even managed a small smile. His grip around my arm loosened a bit and I shook my appendage free. He was too surprised to notice.

It was the perfect time for dashing off, but I suddenly felt the need to take my mother along too. I moved back a few steps. I decided to let the argument go on a bit more and then grasp the opportunity. I didn't care if it was a good decision or not. I just wanted my mother along with me. And I wanted to see my mother standing up to my father.

"I have had quite enough. You have never really treated him like your son. Each person should be allowed to chase his dreams. And it is my responsibility, as his mother, to destroy any obstacles in his way." She drew herself to her full height of five feet four inches and glared at my father dangerously.

My jaw dropped to the floor. I had never heard her speak like that to anyone, leave alone Candling. Apparently, neither had Eternal Cribbing! He looked as if she had just slapped him hard across his face.

I wanted to keep watching, but a small voice at the back of my brain said - *You forgot to take money, you pea-brain! You are going to need it. Don't just stand and gape.*

'Oh, c'mon! Just a few minutes more!'

Then you can starve and die.

'But this is the first time something like this has happened!'

Right, so when you are out in the streets dying of hunger, you can remember the memory of your parents fighting and fill your stomach.

'Fine, you win.'

I inched away slowly. Once I was out of earshot, I bolted to my room, grabbed a small bundle of money. Then I went to my mother's room and grabbed a few clothes for her too. I rushed down to the kitchen after that. I packed in everything edible that was within my reach. I also took a bottle of water. Then, I rushed to my room, took my wallet and stuffed it inside my pocket. I rushed back to the corridor.

"...you have proved what a bad father you can be. Let the boy go his own way. Who are you to stop him? If you really care about him, then just let him go."

"Let him be? Do you even know what you are talking about?"

"Yes, I do. He's sixteen years old. He's old enough to make his own decisions by now. My son wants to become a singer. He is talented. Let him become what he wants."

It was the perfect moment to make my move. I ran down the passageway with my suitcase and my guitar.

I grabbed my mother and bolted. My mother let out a gasp of surprise. What Candling did was a cross between a yell and a snort.

I pulled my mother towards the door. By now, all the maids and butlers in our mansion had started gathering around. Of course, it is only natural to do so; I mean to say: Who in their right mind will miss such a classic quarrel?

I tugged my mother along. Candling was behind us and very close to us as well- I could tell he was debating in that puny mind of his what to do with us.

At the spur of the moment, I decided what I would do. I allowed him to come closer. He opened his mouth, about to yell at us until we lost our ears. I'm not saying that it was a logical decision. I barely had time to think things through. Adrenaline rushed into me. I lifted my suitcase and whacked him right across that silly face of his with it. There was a sick crunching noise. He staggered back in surprise, blood streaming from his nose. I started running, but my mother stopped in her tracks. I stopped too and shot her a questioning look. Her eyes had started tearing up. My forehead wrinkled and I asked her what happened.

"I...cannot leave with you. Please understand, Lewis! I understand why you wish to take me away from here, but I cannot come."

I put my hands on her shoulders and asked, "Why? You will leave this place. This is your chance to start a better life. Come with me, Mother."

Meanwhile, Candling had quickly recovered from the blow. He was a retired Colonel from the army; he was used to wounds like this. He yelled, "Fine! I give up! You may leave the house now, Candling, but your mother stays here."

"Over my corpse," I growled. I pulled her towards the door again. She pleaded, "Please, Lewis. I know your intentions are good, but I cannot come with you."

"And why can't you?" My voice rang around the passageway. "Why in the name of Lucifer can't you?" Tears started streaming down her fair cheeks. I wiped them away with my palms and hugged her. She only came up to my chest. I was suddenly surprised to see how short she was; I literally towered over her.

She sobbed and said, "Because...because...I'm bound by duty." I looked at her as if she had just expressed a desire to jump off the top of Mount Everest screaming 'I love Vivien Leigh'. She opened her mouth to say something, but she was interrupted by the sudden sound of Candling coughing and hacking. I had never seen him like that. Mother immediately ran to his side. I couldn't believe my eyes.

She encouraged, "Go ahead, Lewis. Go and fulfil your dreams. You don't need me by your side to do that. But before you go, just listen to this: All his life, your father has only wished the very best for you. Believe it or not..."

After saying that, she pointed to me, then to the door and smiled. I couldn't manage to fathom the meaning of what she said, but I shot her one last warm look, and without even a glance at my father, I ran out of the door, with my suitcase and guitar in my hands, straight into the world.

Chapter 2

Clark's Inn

I was standing smack in the middle of the street, my mouth wide open in shock. I was taking in everything that was around me. There were so many buildings! I saw a few houses, an inn, a church and a few shops. I had never soaked all of this in before, but I suppose that when you leave your house you start noticing things.

PEEP!!! PEEP!!! PEEP!!!

I looked around sharply after hearing the loud noises of horns. I saw a few cars and an equal number of angry drivers. I had been so fascinated by everything around me that I had forgotten where exactly I was standing. I apologised to them and ran over to one side, trying not to hear the insults they were throwing at me.

After they went off on their own merry ways, I looked around myself once more. I was standing right in front of an inn-the same one I had seen when I was in the middle of the road. It was a huge building, with two wings stretching out in opposite directions and a huge oak front door. A sign over the door read: Clark's Inn. I needed a temporary place to stay, and the inn looked quite decent. So, I took a deep breath and knocked on the door.

The door was opened almost immediately. A tall man who looked like he was in his early forties stood before me. He was in a simple black suit. His face was tanned and scarred. He looked rather rugged; I was sure he belonged to the group of people that can win any fight-physical or mental. His almond-shaped eyes were quite kind. He smiled at me in the kind way that people use to greet their nephews and let me in.

I stepped into a room that was a cross between a living room and a lounge. It was quite spacious and roomy inside. There were many windows, so the place was bright as well. The floor was panelled with wood and all the furniture was polished. A fire roared in the grate. A few people were sitting about and chatting. A smell of cigar smoke lingered in the air. It was altogether a rather homely place.

I heard a cough behind me. I turned around sharply. The man who had brought me inside smiled at me again and pointed to the reception desk. It was towards the far end of the room. I smiled weakly and started walking, my guitar and suitcase in my hands. I reached the desk and stood in the queue behind a family. The man of the family was currently talking to the woman behind the desk. I was quite close, so I could hear the conversation between the woman and a boy, who was evidently her son. He looked about sixteen; my age. He had jet-black hair that was slightly wavy. His eyes were hazel. They looked rather mischievous, but I could also see a wise and a dignified light in them. He was smiling at his mother.

"This seems like a wonderful place, doesn't it, Frank?" the woman asked. I realised with a jolt that her son, Frank, looked exactly like her. They had the same eyes and the same hair, except his mother's hair was elbow-length. Even their complexions were identical. She smiled back at Frank and ruffled his hair. At that moment, I had a sudden desire to look like my mother [I know it was rather silly]. Mothers always seem so understanding, kind, warm and gentle. You can pour your life's worries onto them, but they smile and make things better for you. And on the materialistic side, they always agree to buy you new things. Fathers, on the other hand...well, let's not go over there. I suddenly felt a pang of home-sickness. I wished my mother were here, holding my hand with her dainty one and talking to me in her sweet way. 'Why in the world didn't she agree to come with me?' I thought. 'She just said that she was 'bound by duty'. What sort of duty? Looking at the way Candling treats her, I don't think she should be dutiful to him. She should have come with me. She could have improved her life so much more. Why did she do that?' "Er...Excuse me, sir!" I was snapped out of my thoughts by the voice of the lady behind the reception desk. I walked closer to the reception desk and cleared my throat. "Would you like a silver, gold or platinum room?" [The platinum rooms were the most spacious and luxurious, but also, of course, the most expensive. The gold rooms were somewhere in between and the silver rooms were the cheapest]

"Er...how about a silver room?" I wanted to go for the cheapest so I could focus my spending on other important things. Also, we Candlings are generally very stingy when it comes to money [I know that I'm bashing my own family here, but I want to tell you the truth].

The receptionist smiled at me and said, "Sure. You may have room 356 on the third floor in the South Wing. It has an attached bathroom and a nice view of the city. The charge is two pounds weekly. Meals will be in the range of twenty five pence to one pound, depending upon how much you order." I nodded, smiled feebly back and said, "I shall be having my meals here." "I hope you enjoy your stay here, sir," she said, as she made a note and handed me a key. I pocketed it and set off for my room.

I walked down the third floor corridor in the South Wing, looking for my room. I was so engrossed in looking for my room that I banged into someone. I staggered back and dropped my suitcase on the carpeted floor. "I'm really very sorry. I didn't mean to bang into you like that," I apologised to the boy I had bumped into. He, like the boy I saw at the reception desk, looked like he was about my age.

He was quite pale and he looked exhausted. His eyes were turquoise in colour. He was a bit taller than me. A flick of his red hair was over his left eye. A book lay at his feet, which sported old Oxford shoes. "I apologise for bumping into you," I asked for his forgiveness again. He smiled back ever so slightly, and said, "Oh, it is fine! It's not your fault. I was the one who was reading while walking." He picked his book up-it was Crime and Punishment-and went on his way. 'Seems like a nice person,' I thought as I picked my suitcase up.

❖❖

I turned the key in the lock and pushed the wooden door open. My gaze swept over my temporary home. It was a small but airy room. Light flooded in through three windows. A bed took up space in the middle. There was a cupboard to the right side and a chest of drawers to the left side of the bed. There was a door right opposite the bed. I smiled and thought, 'I love it.'

I set my suitcase and guitar on the bed and removed my coat, tie, shoes and socks. I wanted my feet, which were hurting slightly, to air out. I walked over to the door that was opposite the bed and opened it. As I expected, it was the bathroom. I could make out that someone had recently spray-perfumed it as it smelled quite nice.

I stepped inside and took a good look at myself in the mirror. I looked...horrible. I also gave out an unpleasant odour of perspiration. I ran a hand through my hair, trying to make it tidier. I was quite unsuccessful. And of course, I had conveniently forgotten to take my comb along. I sighed and decided to look after my [in my opinion, fantabulous] hair later. I closed the door, walked over to my bed and sat down. I unclasped my suitcase and took my wallet out of it. I opened it and counted the money inside. I had fifty one pounds and twenty six pence. 'I've got enough money for seventeen weeks, but that does not mean that I do not need a job. I'll go through some newspapers later today and see if I can find one. I need money to support my basic needs as I will pursue my dream,' I thought. Suddenly, my stomach growled far too loudly than was polite. I smiled slightly and put my wallet away. I took a look at my watch and saw that it was ten past one. 'I wonder what's for lunch,' I thought, as I got up to change my clothes.

Chapter 3

LUNCH...AND A FEW PLANS

I stepped into the dining room, clad in a white silk shirt, black trousers, black blazer and a tie. All the tables in the dining room were occupied. I groaned inwardly. I looked around the room for one last time. Suddenly, I caught sight of the boy I had banged into earlier in the day. He was sitting alone, still buried in his book. He was dressed in a simple white button-down shirt and black trousers. I took a deep breath and walked over to him. "Do you mind if I sit here?" I asked. I'm quite well-mannered, don't you think? [Wink wink]. He looked up at me. His flick was still over his eye.

"Er...sure, of course not," he replied. I smiled at him in gratitude and sat down rather elegantly. He shut his book with a slight bang and turned to the waiter who had come to take our order. "I'll have some bread and the onion and turnips stew, please," said the red-haired boy in front of me. The waiter noted his order down and then turned to me. I cleared my throat, took a good five minutes looking at the menu card and then said, "I'll go for the roast turkey and salad. And please fetch the chocolate blancmange too."

I looked back at the boy after the waiter left. He was looking at me with his eyebrows raised. I immediately cocked one of mine and he looked down, flushing. I got the feeling that he wasn't going to strike up a conversation with me any time soon, so I said, "So, what's your name?" He gulped and continued looking down at the table. I decided to put him at ease and said, "Hey, you can relax. I'm not going to eat you up. A whole roast turkey is waiting for me." The boy finally looked up and stuttered, "Oh, y-yes! My-my name i-is Jay." I introduced, "I am Lewis." He nodded once and continued to read. He reminded me a lot of Tyrone Fields, a classmate of mine in school. Tyrone always had his rather broad nose buried in a book.

"Please excuse me, Jay, but may I ask you a few questions about yourself? I assure you, I won't invade too much upon your privacy."

"Oh, ask away. Ask me about anything you like."

I cocked an eyebrow again. I had been with him for less than fifteen minutes and he was ready to tell me about his life. I also felt slightly guilty. I said, "Well, you can ask me anything too, though I will ask you to kindly put a lid on it if it gets too personal for my taste." I managed to flash him a small smile. He smiled back. Slight dimples formed on his pale cheeks. There was something poignant in that smile of his. I started feeling quite awkward. The guilty feeling inside me multiplied. I said, "It is fine. We probably shouldn't be spouting out the stories of our lives after meeting each other so soon." He nodded and returned to Fyodor Dostoyevsky again. Strangely, he looked almost disappointed. I was rather puzzled. It was as if he had bottled up something inside himself and wanted to let it out. I looked down at the table, pretending to be extremely interested in my plate.

"Have you ever lost someone you love?"

I looked up sharply and said, "Excuse me?"

He blushed and replied, "N-Nothing! D-Don't b-b-bother. I-I think I'll l-leave now." He stood up, and before I could do anything to stop him, literally fled from there. I stood up too to follow him, but sat down just as fast for my food, or rather *our* food, had arrived. I started off on my turkey, thoroughly puzzled. It somehow seemed to me as if I had bumped into altogether another person up on the third floor.

After finishing my lunch, I requested a waiter to pack Jay's food. I thought, 'I'll hand it to him. The bloke ran off without having even a morsel.' He had also left his book behind, so I decided to return that too. The packed food arrived after a few minutes. I picked up the package and his book and set off to find Jay. I decided to go to the South Wing on the third floor first because I figured that as I had bumped into him there, he was most likely to be on that floor.

I finally reached my destination. There were nine rooms, excluding my own, along the Wing. I made up my mind to go knock on the door of each of the rooms. After meeting a shy girl who was about half my size, having a not-so-pleasant chat with a drunken man who insisted that I was his son and getting confronted by a very fat lady brandishing a saucepan, I finally found Jay. He was in Room No. 354.

I stood just outside his room and he took up space in the doorway. He looked at me and sighed softly. "You didn't eat any of your food and you forgot your book. See, I got them for you," I said, holding out the parcel and the book. Gratitude rushed into his blue-grey eyes. He took them from my hands and said, "T-Thank you s-s-so much, L-Lew, f-for bringing my f-food and b-b-book to me. I... owe you." I just said, "Don't mention it." I turned on my heel and walked towards my room. On a whim, I decided to go down to the half living room-half lounge and look for a job offers in the newspapers that lined the newspaper stand there. I turned on my heel again [I quite like doing that] and started going in the direction of the living room-lounge.

❖❖

I was sitting on a couch in the 'entrance room', as I began calling it [living room-lounge sounds stupid, doesn't it?]. There was a newspaper in my hands and about thirty more on my lap and beside me. Up until now, two offers had caught my eye and I had set the newspapers that contained those two offers aside. Both of them required the applicant to know fluent English [which I do], be quite good at calculations [which I am] and know typing [I had typed many a times on the typewriters at the Candling Mansion, so there was no problem there too]. Right then, I saw an advertisement in the paper I was currently holding. It said:

HUDSON DISCO LOUNGE

MUSICIAN NEEDED. HE/SHE SHOULD BE BETWEEN 15 AND 21 YEARS. HE/SHE SHOULD BE EDUCATED AT LEAST UNTIL THE CERTIFICATE EXAMINATION. ANY ASPIRING APPLICANTS SHOULD BE AT THE ADDRESS GIVEN BELOW AT ANY TIME BETWEEN ONE O' CLOCK AND FIVE O' CLOCK ON 21ST APRIL.

TIMING OF SHOWS: SEVEN O' CLOCK TO TEN O' CLOCK

SALARY: 50 PENCE PER SHOW

ADDRESS: 17, MORTON LANE, LONDON.

I was so happy that I could have jumped up and started performing a jig in joy. I was good at English and Math and I knew typing, but music was something I excelled at. And as for the Certificate Examinations, I had done quite well. I smiled widely and returned the rest of the papers to the newspaper stand. I went to the reception and asked for a small piece of paper and a pen. After getting those two things, I jotted down the details of each advertisement. I returned the pen to the lady behind the desk, thanked her, pocketed the paper on which I had written down the details, went to the couch, sat down on it, hands behind my head and relaxed for a bit. I was grinning from ear to ear. I had found three advertisements. The date was the 19th of April.

My first interview was on the day after. My Hudson Disco Lounge interview was on the same day as my interview with *London Times Magazine.* And my third interview, which was with Messrs. Burke and Tomlinson Law Firm, was on the day after that. I closed my eyes and imagined myself landing all three of the jobs I was going to be interviewed for.

Chapter 4

Shopping, an Interview and a Hor-rid Shock

I walked down Ashton Street, bags filled with necessities in my hands. I had spent two whole pounds on my shopping. My shopping list looked something like this:

Tooth-brush [Soft]

Tooth-paste [Rotten teeth aren't very nice]

Razor [Beards and moustaches are uncomfortable and they get in the way]

Shaving cream [I don't want the skin covering my cheek-bones to peel off]

Hollywood Romeo Brilliantine [For modern readers; basically shampoo. I know that it is American, but it gets sold in England too and I like it]

Soap [Not the one that airs on radio, the one that helps us clean our bodies]

Comb [My hair is my pride and joy]

Brylcreem [I like to style my waves]

Punch [I love it when my shoes shine]

Notepads [Reader, I expect you to know the reason behind the usage of notepads]

Folder [You know]

Standard Stationary [You know]

Fair papers [For my resume, of course]

Medical necessities [There's always a chance of me getting hurt or falling ill]

Tawn Cologne Deodorant [Come on! I like to smell good. Or rather the reek of sweat makes me feel like vomiting my insides out]

3 Musketeers [Name one person on this planet who doesn't like candy]

I turned into Van Carl Lane and walked towards Clark's Inn. I was busy thinking about my interviews which were on the next day. I continued walking; my head still high up in the clouds. I started whistling an old gypsy tune my mother had taught me when I was little. I was so lost in my day-dreams [I know, I know, I day-dream a lot] that I walked right past the inn. I was about twenty yards away from the gate when I realised that I had come too far. I turned on my heel [I seriously seem to have an obsession with doing that] and started moving towards the inn when I felt a hand on my shoulder. I turned sharply [on my heel again]. Jay stood before me. His hair was tousled and his eyes looked extremely fatigued. His flick, however, was still over his eye. His white shirt was partly tucked inside his trousers. He also gave out an unpleasant odour. I couldn't exactly place what he smelled of, though the pong reminded me of medicines. In short, he looked terrible.

"Um...hi-de-ho, Jay," I greeted. He sighed in such a depressed manner that I felt like putting an arm around his shoulders and comforting him.

"Please may I walk with you?" Jay asked.

"Of course! And there's no need to 'may' me," I replied. He still looked uneasy, though. We started walking in the direction of the inn. "So..." I said, making an attempt to strike up a conversation with the boy walking beside me. "For how long are you going to stay at Clark's Inn?"

He ran a hand through his already dishevelled hair and replied, "I...don't know."

"That's fine. Even I don't know for how long I am going to reside at Clark's." He looked at me, his eyes wide in surprise. I looked at him, my eyes asking him what was so curious about me doing that. He blinked and looked away.

I shrugged and decided to leave his rather odd behaviour aside for a while.

After that, I tried to make conversation with him many times, but he always either ignored me or answered with monosyllable replies. We finally reached the South Wing of the third floor.

"Thank you for walking with me, Lewis," he said, before darting off to his room. I could just stare as he entered his room and shut the door behind him.

❖❖

After a hearty dinner that consisted of roast beef, onion soup and salted and peppered potatoes, I was lying eagle-spread on my bed. I sighed and got off the bed to go and brush my teeth after I heard a clock strike nine. I had decided to go to bed early, so I could wake up nice and fresh in the morning. And anyway, I was feeling quite sleepy. I entered the bathroom and started undressing. I finished brushing my teeth, stepped into my room and practically pounced on my bed. I pulled the covers over my body and kept on moving my head until I found the most comfortable spot on the pillow. I sighed and closed my eyes. 'What a day it has been and tomorrow is a big day,' I thought drowsily as I slowly slipped into the realms of sleep.

❖❖

I was standing outside the manager's office in Hudson Disco Lounge with my guitar strapped to my shoulder. I was dressed in a sky blue shirt, a black coat and black trousers. I didn't have a tie on as I did not want my employer to think that I was overly formal. My hair was combed down quite neatly [though not, of course, in the Edward Candling style] and I had put on plenty of deodorant. [Plenty, actually, is the understatement for the amount of deodorant that had disappeared from the bottle] The resume I had created [truthfully] the day before was in my hand. I was quite nervous and I kept on checking the time in my Omega. [For all those who don't know; my watch]

"Next!" The sound of the voice of the manager almost made me jump out of my skin. I gulped, flattened my hair slightly with my hand and entered the office.

The office was a medium-sized room with a carpeted floor and big windows. Shelves and cabinets lined the walls and a ceiling fan was rotating away. There was a teakwood desk in the middle of the room. Posters of musical heroes covered the walls. And behind the table, with a welcoming smile on his face, was the manager.

The manager was quite young; twenty-six at the most. He was tall, strapping and muscular. He wore a bright silver suit with rainbows on it. [Yes, reader, your eyes do not deceive you] His blond hair was messy and his brown eyes were twinkling mischievously.

"Sit, please," he said, gesturing towards the chair in front of his desk. I went, my knees trembling slightly, towards the chair and sat down.

"I trust you have your resume with you."

I walked out of the other door of the office, feeling jubilant. My interview had gone very well. I had answered all of the manager's questions. He had been quite pleased with me. He had even asked me to sing softly, and I had done that, while playing my guitar. After I had finished, he had clapped loudly. In a nutshell, I had bagged the job.

I walked down Morton Lane, whistling with joy. I was happier than I had ever been in my whole life of sixteen years, and that's saying something. I had a wide grin plastered on my face. Suddenly, I felt the urge to sing. So, I started singing 'April in Paris' with gusto. Pedestrians and shop-keepers stared at me as if I had left my brain in the loo or something. But I did not care at all.

I was practically bouncing when I turned into Van Carl Lane. Suddenly, I stopped short. Something was wrong. Something was definitely amiss. I looked around and what I saw made me want to run to the Candling Mansion and hug my mother. [This is not the time to call me a Mama's Boy] People were standing in front of Clark's, around fifteen feet away from the inn. Traffic had been stopped. Children were wailing and screaming and I could see that one or two women had swooned. There was complete commotion on the lane. I moved a little closer. The unpleasant odour of smoke entered my nostrils.

The inn was engulfed by tall flames.

Chapter 5
Flames

I couldn't believe my eyes. I didn't *want* to believe my eyes. I was so stunned that I couldn't move a muscle. I heard the voice of the receptionist saying, "I've called the fire brigade. They should be here any moment now." I suddenly felt a hand on my shoulder. Jerked out of my stay-still-and-stare reverie, I turned around [on my heel]. I saw the man who had first opened the doors of the inn for me.

He said, in a rather gruff voice, "I don't see your pal here, son." His words sent a shiver down my back, partly because I had never heard him speak before and his voice was a bit scary and partly because I thought I had quite a good idea of whom he was referring to. He spoke, "I haven't seen that redheaded twangie-boy since we ordered evacuation."

"Then why isn't he being searched for?" I asked.

"The firemen are on their way, lad. They will look for him."

I said, my voice cracking a bit, "So you're just going to stand here and do nothing. What if he's severely burnt by the firemen arrive, or even worse, dead?" I didn't know why, but Jay was starting to grow on me. The man beside me had gone off into the crowd. I stamped my foot in a frustrated state. Then, a very brave but equally 3.141 [irrational] thought entered my brain.

I slowly backed away from the mob of people. Luckily, no one saw me. I ran slowly along the wall of the front-yard of the inn and climbed over it not-so-lithely. I fell smack on my behind in one of the inn's flower-beds. I think I squashed some daisies and chrysanthemums. I stood up quickly and tried to brush some petals off the rear of my trousers.

Oi, air-head! Save the boy and leave your damn rear alone.

Aah...my inner voice again.

I did as it instructed me to. I ran around the inn, looking for a way to enter the inn. Reader, you may have read some stories in which the hero always finds a way into the burning building and saves whoever that is inside. But it appeared as if fate and destiny did not want me to be lucky in the story they were writing together.

I went to the back door and tried to open it by force, but it was of no use. Finally, I picked up a small-sized rock I found in the garden and chucked it at a back window. As expected, the glass shattered instantly. Without thinking twice, I climbed in. My shin scraped against a shard of glass that was still stuck in the window-frame. I fell flat down on the floor of a room, clutching my leg. The shard had created a long cut on my right shin. But I had other things on my mind. I staggered to my feet and limped towards the door. Half the room was on fire. There were plenty of magazines on the bed that caused the fire to spread quickly. Cursing the owner of the room in my mind, I opened the door and entered the corridor. The good thing: I wasn't greeted by unfriendly flames. The bad thing: Both ends of the corridor were on fire, so I couldn't go anywhere from there. I decided to check Jay's room first. Luckily, the staircase wasn't on fire. I started climbing up the steps. I was currently in the North Wing.

'I'll first have to get to the third floor. Then, I'll get to the South Wing and check that fool's room,' I thought. I finally got to the third floor of the North Wing. It was almost untouched by the flames. Crossing my fingers,

I started limping as quickly as I could towards the South Wing.

❖❖

I practically ricocheted off the third floor of the South Wing. It was completely and totally on fire. Red-hot flames had *owned* the whole floor. I wanted to go back that second. I wanted to save my own life. I didn't want to die all because of some stupid boy.

So...backing off, are we?

'Hey! I'll die if stay here any longer!'

So will Jay. Do you want to run away, Lewis? Do you want to leave a young boy to his death?

'He can also be in some other place, you know. And I'm young too, in case you haven't noticed.'

But what if he's in his room, unable to protect himself? I'm asking you again, do you want to leave a young boy to his death? Do you want to be selfish and save just your own life? Do you not care about him? Do you want to show the world what a big coward you are? And is 'I'm young too' your excuse for not saving a life?

Suddenly, I got hit by a wave of fury. 'I am *not* a coward,' I thought. 'And I *will* save Jay.' With those two thoughts in my mind, I went straight into the evil flames.

❖❖

I was choking. I couldn't breathe. Half of my brain was telling me that I should just let it be and save myself. The other half, however, was urging me to continue. Coughing and retching, I moved in the direction of Jay's room. I finally reached it and saw that the door had almost burnt away. I pushed through the burnt remains of what was once a strong partition between a room and a corridor and entered Jay's room.

Flames had come up to his bed and they were threatening to reach their fiery arms further. I ran to the part of his room that was not burning. I took a good look at the room. Almost half of its floor was on fire. Flames had now started licking Jay's bed. And, on the bed was Jay himself. He was laying eagle-spread, his eyes shut tightly and his chest rising and falling in a strange pattern.

I suddenly felt another wave of anger hit me. I ran over to him and shook him hard. He did not budge. "Get up, you idiot! By Lucifer, the inn's on fire and I'm suffering because of you!" I yelled into his ear. He still did not move. And then I smelled it-the horrible reek of sleeping pills and knockout drops. The lad was practically surrounded by empty bottles! I was stunned. I had never heard of it before- a teenage boy taking so many sleeping pills and pain medicines.

Move, now! You cannot afford to get paralysed.

I shook my head vigorously, trying to shake off the smell of the medicines and the sight of Jay lying surrounded by so many bottles. I put one of my hands under his thighs and the other one just below his shoulders and picked him up.

"Oof!" I exclaimed. For a boy so thin, Jay was surprisingly heavy. So, I let his feet touch the floor. I debated on what to do next. One look at the fire and I knew that we wouldn't get through it alive. The windows were an option, but we were on the *third* floor and the ground below the window was made of asphalt [just our luck!]. There was no way I could jump down with Jay. I tried to form a quick escape plan, but the heat of the fire was making my brain function particularly slowly. I hit my head in frustration. I could either take us through the fire and kill us both, or jump out one of the windows and kill us both. Suddenly, on the spur of the moment, I decided to take one of the windows. I have no idea even today what exactly induced me to make the choice. I get these strange hunches sometimes. [Now, please don't name me the Hunchback of Notre Dame] I dragged Jay over to the window. I opened it and took Jay on my back. I caught the top-rail and swung my leg with difficulty over the sill. I looked down and what I saw made me want to jump to the sky with joy. The firemen had arrived.

I had never been so happy to see anyone before. I yelled out from the window and the firemen immediately set up two ladders. One fireman climbed up on each. I handed Jay over to the fireman that had come to the window we were by, moved as quickly as I could to the other window and threw it open. The fireman over there took me in his arms and slowly climbed down the ladder.

That was some good work, Lewis.

'Glad you're proud.' [My thoughts dripping with sarcasm]

Hahaha!

I wanted to think up something clever to say, but I could not do so, for, at that very moment, I felt my head spin and I fainted.

I finally came to after goodness-only-knows how much time. Sparks were doing a wild jig in front of my eyes. My stomach was lurching horribly and I had a nasty headache. In a nutshell, I felt quite terrible. After about five minutes, my condition improved slightly. I propped myself up on my elbows and swept my gaze over my surroundings.

I was on a bed in what looked like a hospital room. There was a small table at my bed-side, on which there was an apple and a jug of water. Feeling very thirsty all of a sudden, I gripped the handle of the jug and pulled it to my lips. Needless to say, I spilled half of the water in it on the patient suit I was attired in. After drinking some of it,

I returned the jug to its place and continued looking around the room I was in. There was another bed by my side. Lying on it was Jay.

When I saw him, I felt really angry. It was all because of him and his dirty habits that I was in that state. After giving him one last livid look, I tore my eyes away from him.

Suddenly, the door of the room opened. A woman dressed in nurse's clothes entered. I looked at her in surprise. When she saw that I was conscious, she came over to my bed and said, "I think you are all right now, boy. However, you will have to stay here for a few more days. Lewis Candling, welcome to Cornwall Naval Defence Camp."

Chapter 6

Meeting Fergusson

I was mortified. My jaw dropped far down. The nurse raised her eyebrows and said, "You have been asked to meet the Commander in twenty minutes. I think you should take a wash and change into some new clothes." She went to a chest of drawers in the corner of the room and pulled out a drab grey shirt and a pair of black trousers. She came to me again and laid the clothes on my bed. Then, she smiled and exited the room.

I couldn't move a muscle. I simply sat there on my bed, thinking about what I had lost. I had lost my clothes. I had lost my money. I had lost some of my other important belongings. I had lost my GUITAR. And I had *almost* lost my life. I simply couldn't process it. Then, I suddenly remembered that some of my mother's clothes had also been there with me. I could have kicked myself. My mother's clothes had just been burned-all because of me. Also, even though she had been very brave, I knew that I had shattered her heart when I announced that I was leaving. She was with an absolutely nightmarish person without her son to help her. I felt like slapping myself across the face.

'Well, I'm going to do something about it, most definitely,' I thought fiercely. 'My poor mother has endured enough. When I'm out of this place, I'm going to go and get her. A good son should stop at absolutely *nothing* to make his mother's world a better place.'

"You are Master Lord Lewis Edward Candling?"

I nodded. I had changed into the clothes the nurse had given me. The Commander put his hand to his chin and looked at me intently. He had dark brown hair and he was tall, strapping, tanned and muscular. He had hazel eyes and high cheek-bones. He said, "You must be wondering how you turned up here."

I nodded again. I wanted to say something, but the Commander was...intimidating, in his own way. Also, he reminded me of someone, but I just could not place whom.

"My name is Commander Daniel Fergusson," he said, "And I will tell you how you got here."

Finally, I spoke. My voice came out slightly shaky. "Please do, sir."

He nodded grimly and began, "You saved a lad from the burning inn, did you not? That was quite a brave deed. After the firemen rescued the two of you from the flames, you fainted. You regained your consciousness here, in our Hospital Wing. The other lad, however, is not so lucky. There are too many medicines inside his body. He will stay out of consciousness for another week or so, according to what the nurses have told me. And, he will probably have high fever when he awakens. But I am not concerned about that right now. By the way, you were brought here by Vice-Admiral Schneider."

"Vice-Admiral Schneider?" I asked, confused.

R.A. Fergusson said, "He retired as Vice-Admiral. Clark's Inn was his. It held fond memories for him. It is a shame it burnt down. Anyway, he thought this would be the best place for you to recover."

"But why here? There are so many hospitals in London. And Cornwall is so far away from London; four hundred and eleven point nine kilometres, to be precise."

Fergusson sighed and said, "This place is the safest one for you to be in at the moment. You see..."

He was cut off by the sound of knocking on the door. "Enter!" Fergusson said.

The door swung open. I was astonished to see who came in. It was Frank, the black haired boy I had seen at the reception on my first day at Clark's Inn.

Fergusson looked at the boy for a moment and then nodded, acknowledging him. He came and stood right beside me. It hit me suddenly why Commander Fergusson seemed so familiar. My surprise must have shown on my face, because Commander Fergusson nodded and said, "Yes, he is related to me. I am his brother."

I got a shock when I heard that. Then it struck me how young Commander Fergusson was. He didn't look a day older than twenty-three. From the corner of my eye, I saw Frank rolling his eyes.

"Can we sit now, your *Low*ness?" He asked.

Commander Fergusson narrowed his eyes and presented his brother with an angry glare. He replied, his voice only slightly warmer than the Antarctic, "I must ask you to be polite, *brother*. I can have you kicked out of here at any moment, straight into the sea, but I am not doing so as I am large-hearted and I care for your worthless life. You should be thankful to me instead of behaving like this."

Frank literally growled and started cursing under his breath. I could make out a few words and phrases here and there like 'fat-head', 'Old Nick', 'ought to have his uprights snapped' and 'twit'.

"So," said R.A. Fergusson, looking pointedly away from his younger brother, "I will explain everything to you. I trust you know who Adolf Hitler is. Well, the thing is th... *what the hell do you think you are doing?*"

Fergusson's face was red with rage. His hands were clasped tightly and on the table. He was glaring furiously at Frank, who whipped around and returned his brother's glare. He had been fingering a rifle kept in his brother's office. "Get out," Fergusson ordered. "Get your sorry self out of my office right now, or else I will not include you in our plan." Frank shot his brother one last vexed look and stormed out of the office, slamming the door behind him.

"That brat needs to be taught some manners. His head is filled with nothing but saw-dust," Fergusson vented his feelings.

This sounded so much like what my mother's sodding husband used to say to me that I was quite surprised for a moment. But then I thought that maybe all people in Defence talked like that. And Fergusson's eyes had kindness in them too; *his* eyes did not have even a speck of it.

Fergusson said, "Now, I can finally begin explaining a few things to you. You know who Adolf Hitler is, right?"

I nodded. Adolf Hitler was a psychopathic German who looked like a clown, according to me.

"Good," Fergusson continued. "You see, he is up to no good. Something is definitely cooking inside that brain of his. Whatever it is can cause massive destruction."

"You mean...something like war may *really* happen?"

"Yes. Churchill and so many others have predicted war. I do not like to say this, but the bloodshed and carnage on this continent did not end with the conclusion of the Great War."

Chapter 7
The Plan

I nodded to myself as I processed all that he had told me. He looked at me. I opened my mouth, about to ask him what my role was in all of this, when a loud gong sounded. The door of the office swung open and a Midshipman peeped in.

"Sir, we have to get to sea immediately. It is an emergency." Fergusson nodded at the Midshipman. The latter left and Fergusson said, "I will explain the rest to you when I get back. Or, if you want to know about our plan badly, you may ask my brother, though I doubt he will relate it to you without any exaggerations. Farewell, Lewis!" With that, he picked his rifle up and rushed out the door.

I walked down the corridor, my hands in the pockets of the trousers I was currently wearing. I turned and came face to face with a dead halibut. What an unpleasant pong! It was hanging from a thin thread. Its insides were carved out in a horrid fashion. I of course, did the natural thing. I backed away from it, my eyes closed tightly and covering my nose with my hand.

"Oh! Dear. He's new here! Don't trick him so. And please put that halibut away."

At that, I opened my eyes. Frank stood right in front of me, the string from which the mutilated fish was hanging in his hand. A pretty young woman stood facing Frank. She was quite tall and very thin. She had long dark brown hair which was braided back and light brown eyes. She was very fair. She looked like she was in her early twenties.

Frank exclaimed, "I was jus' checking his nut!"

The woman said, "Please throw it away. It's giving out a really horrid smell."Frank went away with his stinking fish.

The woman turned to me and said, "Hello! Your name is Lewis, isn't it?" I nodded. She smiled sweetly at me, held out a hand and said, "My name is Eva Carter. I am the Head Army Doctor at Cornwall Naval Defence Camp."

I smiled back and shook her hand. After a few pleasantries were exchanged, I asked her, after hesitating for a second or two, "Please may I know how Jay is?"

"Oh, do you mean the red-haired boy?" Dr. Carter asked.

When I nodded in reply, she said, "He is breathing well and his pulse is very close to normal. He will recover, but it will be painful for him. He has ingested many pain medications. He may have a high temperature when he regains his consciousness. He might also have a splitting headache and most probably nausea too. But you don't need to worry about him, Lewis, he will recover. And two of my best assistants are watching over him. He will come to in about a week."

"Yes, Commander Fergusson told me that."

"Did he also tell you that that boy's name is not Jay but Sir Martin Jeremy Esquire and that he is Heir to the Duke of Leicester?"

"What?!" I was flabbergasted. [Reason number one: He was Heir to the Duke of Leicester. Reason Number two: He had never really acted like he was a Duke's son whenever he was around me. It was just...unbelievable.]

"It's true."

I just stood there, unable to believe what she had just told me. At that moment, Frank appeared next to us. "I gave it the honey cooler of a farewell, Dr. Carter."

She smiled at him and said, "Very good. Now, I really must be going. I have to check on all the patients." She waved at us and went off.

I turned to Frank and asked, "Please will you tell me what the plan is?"

He nodded and said, "I will pal, but after mess. I'm absolutely dying for some albatross."

I was sitting beside Frank. We weren't allowed to go outside the main building, so we had to make do with being indoors. Both of us were munching on bars of chocolate. [I know that such amounts of chocolate weren't usually available at Defence Camps, but the cook had made a huge stock, and some bars were left over] I reminded, "You were going to tell me what the plan is."

He swallowed some chocolate and said, "So I did. And I'll bunny it to you this minute."

I looked at him expectantly. Frank began, "A few weeks ago, our fathers hacked into that Turd of a Hitler's personal records. You see, they entered Hitler's camp in disguise, with backpacks and a whole lot of explosives in them. Y'know, the Germans aren't half as clever as we think they are."

"Hmm," I said, gesturing to him to continue.

So, they secretly made their way to Hitler's tent. The soldiers guarding it asked to see their I.Ds, which had been forged by them. Of course, no one suspected a thing. They came out a while after that. The next thing the Germans knew, their leader's tent was blown up by one of our party. The whole affair was quite hush-hush, of course. But that Abercrombie of a brother prattled out the story to me. And, well, our paters were almost caught and done off with. Hitler's furious- he wants to kill our fathers and the rest of our families for revenge, or 'rache', as they call it in their stupid language. So, obviously, they have to keep their families all safe and sound now. Clark's Inn was the hide-out place for us. I got transported there, my identity changed, along with my brother and cousin sister dressed as my parents. Now, *that* was one awkward affair. It's lucky that I look just like my cousin."

I was mortified. Frank, on the other hand, looked quite calm and composed. I swallowed several times, trying to get over the fact that Hitler was looking for us. Frank put his hand on my shoulder comfortingly and said, "You'll get over it; I did." I wiped my brow with the sleeve of my shirt. He soothed, "Nothing will happen to your family or to you. Trust me. You're quite safe here." I took several deep breaths, trying to calm myself.

I immediately said the first thing that came to my mind, "B-But I have to go and get my mother! I..."

"I'm sorry, pal, but you can't."

"What happens to our mothers?"

"Well, I don't know about that. It hasn't been shared yet with me. And anyway, it's 'your mater', not 'our maters'."

My brow creased as I looked at him questioningly. He sighed and said, "Look, she's...she's not alive, alreet? She died while giving birth to me." I stared at him. I couldn't believe life without a mother. "I'm sorry."

"Don't be." There was an awkward silence. "That's why he hates me." I looked up and raised my eyebrows. He met my eyes with his sad ones and said, "My brother loved-and still loves-our mater very much. According to him, she died because of me."

"That's not fair."

"I suppose it isn't, then. But I think he *is* justified to think that way. After all, his joy burst like a bubble that day." There was another silence. After about five minutes, he said, "But I've got to forget all of that and get on with my life, I guess." He managed a small smile. I couldn't help but marvel at him.

Wanting to change the topic, I asked, "So...your name isn't Frank?"

"'Course not," he replied, stretching his legs out. "My actual name is William- William Patrolman Fergusson. But please call me Will."

"So only your brother was in disguise. But why didn't they disguise you and your cousin?"

He replied, "Well, the German authorities know me by name, but not by face- my brother told me that. As for my sister, she's come to England for a vacation. Her place is in Spain."

"I comprehend."

Will nodded and continued, "Well, so we reached the hide-out. To be frank, [WILL INTENDED NO PUN] I almost flipped my wig when I saw you just like that, without any escort. We would have been in quite a spot of trouble, if I hadn't practiced acting so fabulously beforehand. You reached the inn by co-incidence, didn't you?"

"I did. I didn't know it was a hide-out. By the way, I just want to ask you something. If my father wanted to ship me to Clark's Inn, why didn't he tell me about the whole plan?"

"Your father is very full of himself, Lewis. He thought that he could keep you safe."

"Yes, when I walked out..."

"YOU WALKED OUT FROM HOME?"

"Er...yes I did."

"Murder!"

"Right...so I was saying, when I ran away, he tried to stop me, but in the end he just let me go."

Will's brow furrowed and he said, "Well, he shouldn't have let you go like that; especially since he was the one who tried to kiss off Hitler."

I didn't know why, but I had been expecting it to be my father. I said bitterly, "That just proves that he is an incarnation of ugly old Lucifer." [But, in my mind, I looked at Edward Candling in a very slightly better light]

Will raised an eyebrow and continued, "So, my crumb of a brother made this brilliant plan. He's going to arrange for us to reach Switzerland. Switzerland is a relatively peaceful place and it has resolved to be neutral if a war begins. Hitler's men won't even dream of looking for us over there. So, I leave for Switzerland in three days' time. You leave after eight days. I'll be going to Zurich and you'll be taking shelter in Geneva. We have to stay in our shelters until the danger has passed. When Hitler finally gets his sorry buttock kicked, we shall come out of our shelters and continue life."

"I have a question. I exited the inn so many times. How was I allowed to do that?"

"Trained people were watching you at all times; the tramps along the roads, for example. They were paid to do it. It was a technique to get them to fight if a war at all begins."

"Oh. But it was a bit too risky, don't you think?"

"Life is all about risk sometimes. And anyway, what the tosh is life without risk?"

"But..."

"They didn't want you to be cooped up inside all day."

"Still..."

"Wouldn't it have looked suspicious to the other lodgers that you didn't get out of that inn at all; at least to that receptionist? She isn't in on all of this."

"But when did my father go and do all that? How come I never got to know?"

Will shook his head and said, "Did you expect your father to say 'Good-bye son, I am going and hacking Hitler's personal records and attempting to kiss him off'?"

I shook my head at my stupidity and asked, "But then you changed your name to Frank, didn't you? How did they allow me to keep my name?"

"Now that's a good question. When you entered the inn, a man from the intelligence dressed as the waiter told the receptionist a fake name for you. He also informed her that the owner had been expecting you. As you didn't know a dicky-bird of the plan, you would have blown everything into smithereens."

"Nice plan," I complimented. "Not 'nice', pal, it was bloody excellent. And by the way, that's why the receptionist didn't ask you your name," he said. I recalled my conversation with her and chided myself mentally for not noticing it before.

"But why are we going all the way to *Switzerland*? Won't Ireland do just as well?"

"Quite the asker of questions, aren't you? Switzerland is quite safe, and so is the route we take to reach it. And Northern Ireland is still a part of the United Kingdom, remember?"

"Hey, but isn't Switzerland Germany's neighbour?"

"It is, but it has resolved to stay neutral. It is quite safe, I assure you. Hitler has sworn not to harm it until the war is done with. And he can't break his promise because he has sworn over the Holy Reich." [If you do not know, the Holy Reich is the sacred book of the Nazis]

"Oh, I understand now."

"Glad you do."

Chapter 8

Hail Lord Ares!

We had just finished dinner, and were going to Will's room. He was sharing it with me, which I thought was quite kind of him. "So, Lew, anything else you want to know?" He asked.

I shrugged and said, "Well, nothing else of importance."

We reached Will's room. He fished a key out of his pocket and opened the door. His room was small, but quite cosy. There was a single bed adjacent to the wall opposite us. A writing table stood to one side and there was a wardrobe opposite to the table. A white carpet covered the floor. Clothes were strewn all over the place. There was a box of unfinished candy on the table. I stepped inside the room. Will followed me, shutting the door behind him. He leaned on the wall and asked, "So...how do you like it?"

I flashed him a small smile and said, "It's brilliant."

He smiled too and went and sat on his bed. He gestured to the spot beside him. I went and sat down on his left. I asked him, "So, where do I sleep?" He replied, "On the bed, of course." I raised my eyebrows and questioned, "But then where are you going to...?"

"I have a foldable mattress in my wardrobe. I'm going to cover that with a sheet and doze off on the floor."

"But won't it be a bit uncomfortable?"

"No, I'll be just fine."

"Are you sure? I mean, I can always exchange places with you, you know."

"Not needed."

I smiled at him in gratitude. I was just going to ask him if I could have some of the candy on the table, when I heard loud barking. And it wasn't just the barking of one dog. It was as if all the dogs in Cornwall had come together and were barking their heads off. I looked at Will, who looked quite vexed.

He got up and went to his wardrobe. He opened it and took something out of it. He shut the doors of his wardrobe, walked to the bed and sat down.

"What's that?" I asked him, curious.

Suddenly, the barking reduced. "I bet my Barnet he's given sedatives to each and every one of them," Will growled, sounding quite like a dog himself.

I felt very bad for the poor creatures, but I didn't want to test Fergusson's patience. "Foolish, sodding, jelly-brained git," Will muttered, showing me what he had gotten from his wardrobe. It was a small and rather thick wooden square. On it was a picture, clearly hand-painted, of a handsome young male. He had a highly tanned complexion and red eyes. Dark curls leaked from his silver war helmet, which had a red plume on top. His cheekbones were quite high. I knew who he was the second I saw him. Lord Ares, the Greek god of war and victory, stared at me from the square. I looked up at Will and asked, "Did you paint this?"

He nodded. "Well, it is very good!" I complimented. He smiled, "Thank you. By the way, soldiers wear a chain of Lord Ares around their necks when they are fighting in battle. They do it for luck, of course."

"Yes, I know that. I saw one like that in *his* room and asked Mother about it." Will smiled at me. I had told him about the rivalry I had against Edward Candling.

He said softly, "Why don't we doss now?"

I woke up the next day to Will slapping my face lightly. My eyes fluttered open and I sat up groggily. I asked him, "Wazzatime?"

He laughed slightly at me and said, in the way a poet presents his piece of work, "It's six on the clock and there are ships in the naval dock!"

"Mrrmmhhhhh..." I said, digging my face into my pillow. My earliest waking-up time was eight o' clock. I just couldn't manage to get out of bed before that. Will started shaking me violently. Just as perseverant, I settled deeper into the bed. After about half a minute, he stopped shaking me.

'*Finally!*' I thought in relief as I started slipping into unconsciousness once again. All of a sudden, a pint of icy water landed on my being. I sat up once more, gasping and spluttering. Will stood right beside the bed, an empty bucket in his hand and a huge grin on his face. "Why, you...!" I leaped out of bed and started chasing him around the room. After a few minutes of running, jumping, stumbling, cursing and Will's laughing, I was forced to accept defeat. He was just too quick for me. I went, grumbling, to the bathroom to get ready for the day.

Breakfast was quite a good affair. It was true that we did not have much variety, but the boiled eggs were well-cooked and the orangeade was delicious. "So," I said, my mouth filled with eggs. "What's the plan for the day?"

Will suggested, "How about this; we'll put ice in my brother's boots." I swallowed and shook my head. "No, he's busy right now. I don't think we should do anything like that to him at a time like this." Will rolled his eyes. I took a swig from my orangeade mug and suggested, "We can go and help out in the NMAD [Naval Medical Aid Department]." He looked at me as if my senses had gone on vacation to the French Riviera or something. Now it was my turn to roll my eyes.

There was a knock on the door. I stood up, got to the door in three strides and opened it; outside stood a nurse. She said, "Commander Fergusson wants to see you at the NMAD main room, Master Lewis." I nodded, looked over my shoulder at Will and said, "I'm going to the NMAD main room." He raised his hands in mock blessing. I rolled my eyes at him and stepped out of the room, closing the door behind me.

The NMAD main room was hustling and bustling with nurses tending to patients. Some of them were administering medicine to sailors that had been victimized by influenza; some were bandaging broken appendages, while others were applying lotion onto wounds. I saw Commander Fergusson sitting in a corner. I walked towards him.

"Good afternoon, Commander Fergusson." He smiled at me and said, "Same to you, Lewis, same to you. Now, do take a seat." I sat down on a chair and looked at him expectantly. "Lewis, about your mother, she is probably in Spain right now. Spain has chosen to stay blissfully neutral. My sister lives there too. She is managing the shelter where your mother will be. I assure you, she is, and will be, absolutely safe. Your father will probably be in the same shelter as her."

I clenched my fists at the mention of Edward Candling, but didn't say anything about him. Instead, I spoke, "I'm glad to hear that." I made to get up, but Fergusson said, "I want to talk to you about another topic."

I raised my eyebrows and asked, "What topic, Commander?"

He sighed and said, "Martin."

Chapter 9

SEPARATION

I got hit by a tidal wave of fury. I gritted my teeth and asked, "What about him?" Commander Fergusson answered, "He has to be transported to a safe place too. But when he wakes up, he will be too weak to go on his own. So, I have decided to send him off to Geneva with you."

I almost fell off the chair I was sitting on. I was royally stunned; and angry. Commander Fergusson said, "Please understand, Lewis. Martin needs someone to be with him. I beg you to try to understand. His past life has not been easy. He needs a friend. I know that you have still not forgiven him, Lewis, but please be considerate. Forgive him. I am sure that you have heard the saying- 'Forgive and Forget'. Lewis, have mercy and forget about that incident. Holding grudges has never helped anyone."

I gripped the side of my chair so hard that my knuckles turned the colour of milk. I said, "Commander Fergusson, I cannot simply '*Forgive* and *Forget*'. Fine, maybe his past life has not been easy. But that is absolutely no excuse for him to start taking drugs. I risked my very *life* to save his sorry one. How can you expect me to pardon him?"

Commander Fergusson laughed bitterly and said, "Lewis, I have risked *my* life to save so many of my fellow sailors. But I have never held anything against any one of them. I have forgiven and forgotten; it is what true soldiers have to do."

Now as I look back on his words, I realise that they held priceless wisdom, but at that time they just added fuel to the fire. I stood up and yelled, "I CANNOT forgive him!

I almost *died* because of his filthy habits. And anyways, you certainly don't practice what you preach, do you? You just said that soldiers have to forgive and forget. Then, why are all of you so bent on war? Why do you all enjoy killing people? Why don't you'll just pardon them and forget about them? And yes, you said that holding grudges has never helped anyone. Then why do you hold such a huge one against your own brother? He wasn't responsible for your mother's death, you know. But you just go on hating him. You know what; I'm going to give you some time to think about all of that. 'Forgive and forget', indeed!" With that, I turned sharply [on my heel, again] and stormed off.

I entered Will's room, slamming the door shut behind me. Will looked up at me. He was crouching beside a huge suitcase, filling clothes in it. I suddenly realised that he was going to leave for Zurich the next day. I walked over to the bed in his room and collapsed on it.

Will asked me, "So, did you have a bit of a ding-dong with him?"

I told him everything that had happened in the NMAD main room, ending with, "You're right, Will. He really *is* thick-skulled."

He smiled and said, "I told you so."

I nodded and asked, wanting to change the subject, "So, you're leaving tomorrow, right?" He said, "Yes, I leave in the afternoon. It's going to be all very hush-hush." I propped myself up on my elbows and said, "Hey, Will." He turned to look at me, his hand about to put a pair of boxers in his suitcase. "I'm going to miss you," I said. He smiled slightly and said, "Same here. But it's fine. Who knows, we may even see each other again after the war."

"I certainly hope so."

"You know, let's meet up after the war. When the war is over, we'll meet right here, in this very room, at precisely nine o' clock on the day after the end of the war. We'll swap notes then!"

"That is, *if* we're alive after the war ends."

"There can be no war at all, you know."

"The chances of that are quite slim. Churchill is expecting one."

"Hey, don't be so miserable. It's going to be fine. Maybe Hitler will get locked inside a refrigerator and freeze to death or something. And to hell with Churchill; he isn't Jesus Christ, you know."

I tried to think in an optimistic way like him, but it was impossible. I reminded him, "Hitler is quite intelligent, Will. He's not going to get locked inside a refrigerator anytime soon."

Will said, "So you're going to keep on thinking negative. I see."

"Well, I, in fact, we all, have to be realistic."

"Not necessary in the least. If you believe that a miracle will occur, and you want it to occur, it will. Now how about we pull a few pranks to lighten up the atmosphere?"

I was standing outside Will's room, waiting for him to come outside. I have to admit, I was feeling a bit sad. I realised with a jolt that chances were that I would never ever see him again. Will was a very different person; he was scared of lightning, [he had told me that over dinner the previous day] but yet he was not afraid of the journey that lay ahead of him. He was very strong, but he did not seem to have the strength to pick a rose from the indoor gardens in the building.

The door opened and Will stepped out. He was dressed in a simple off-white shirt and grey trousers. Over that shirt he wore a simple coat. He had apparently not shaved, because I could see a little bit of stubble on his cheeks. His hair was combed neatly and I could clearly make out the scent of cologne emanating from him. There were two suitcases in his hands. He grinned at me, showing off his perfect teeth. He punched me playfully on the arm and we started walking towards Commander Fergusson's office, where we would part.

The journey lapsed in silence. Only when we reached the door of Fergusson's office was it broken. "So, this is it," Will said.

"I'm going to miss you, mate," I muttered.

"I too, pal. Hey, listen to this. We may or may not meet again; that only fate can decide. But just don't forget that you knew a chap named Will, fine?"

I smiled at him and clapped him on the shoulder. He grinned back and shoved his hand into the left-side back pocket of his trousers. He took out the painting of Lord Ares he had made and offered it to me. I accepted it from him and said, "Hi-de-ho, Will, thanks for this!" He bowed mock-regally and I just had to laugh.

Suddenly, he lunged at me and enveloped me in a rib-crushing hug. He left me after a good minute. I gasped for breath, massaged my front and said, "A small tip for you, Will. Next time you hug someone, try not to crack their ribs."

He simply smiled and said, "Good-bye, Lewis. It was nice knowing you."

I nodded and said, "It was wonderful knowing you too. So long, Will."

He winked, gave a quick two-fingered salute, opened the door of his brother's office and disappeared behind it, leaving me staring at the small picture of Lord Ares he had painted.

Chapter 10
Departure

It has been said by many that time flies like an arrow, but after Will left, it seemed to be travelling extra slowly. Now that he was gone, I had no one to talk to. The other males in the camp were all older than me and were always busy, the nurses would have nothing to do with me and Commander Fergusson had made it his mission in life to give me the royal ignore. The only plus point of Will's departure was that I had his room all to myself.

I could be found sitting around on his bed and reading the few books he possessed. I exited his room only for meals. At nights, I tossed and turned, thinking about my mother and how she was. Time dragged on; for the first time in my life, I felt glad when the time to pack my bag came. I stuffed in exactly nine pairs of trousers, about the same number of shirts and a few coats. I even threw in one or two ties. A few suits followed. I also threw in the painting of Lord Ares Will had given me.

Finally, I finished packing. I flopped down onto the bed, tired. I ran my hands through my wavy hair, breathing deeply. I did not want to travel with Martin in the least, but I decided to co-operate. And, as much as I hated to admit it, I was still concerned about Martin's life despite the burning inn incident.

I took a good look at the room I had lived in for the past few days. I doubted whether I would be entering it ever again. I dressed in a simple suit with a travelling cloak on top. In my hands I carried my bag. A hat rested on my head at a slight angle. I took a deep breath in, opened the door and let myself out.

I walked to Commander Fergusson's office. I dreaded going there, because I was sure that he would still be angry with me. In a few minutes, I was outside the door of his office. I squared my shoulders, gulped and knocked on his door.

"Come in!" I heard Commander Fergusson shout from inside the office. I pushed the door open [I used my back] and entered the office. I saw Commander Fergusson sitting behind his desk, in his naval uniform and with a pair of spectacles on the bridge of his long nose. On the other side of the desk were two chairs; one of which was occupied by the red-haired Martin.

He was dressed in a plain white shirt, navy-blue trousers and a beige travelling coat. His skin was pale and flaxy and he looked exhausted. His hands were shaking slightly. His droopy eyes had a tinge of red in them and glistened with water. He was rather green in the face, as if he had been sick for the whole morning. He was sweating profusely. In a nutshell, he looked like a rotten pretty-boy.

I gritted my teeth and looked away from him quickly. I was sure that if I looked at him for too long, I would break his legs and I certainly didn't want to have a court case on my head. There was an awkward silence in the room, which was broken a few minutes later by Commander Fergusson clearing his throat. I braced myself for the long lecture that would surely escape Commander Fergusson's lips.

However, to my surprise, he did nothing of the sort. Instead, he asked politely, "Aren't you going to take a seat, Lewis?"

Bamboozled, I placed my bag against the one of the walls adjacent to the door and stood up straight to face Commander Fergusson. "Sit down, Lewis," Commander

Fergusson said, gesturing towards the empty chair beside Martin's. I clenched and unclenched my fists and walked over to the chair and plopped down. I may have done that a bit too heavily, because the chair collapsed under me, my being on top of it.

I got up, thoroughly embarrassed. I set the chair on its four legs again and sat down as lightly as a feather. Commander Fergusson's eyebrows were raised and Martin was staring at me. There was another awkward silence, which was again broken by Commander Fergusson. "So, Lewis, are you ready with everything?" He asked. I nodded in reply. Commander Fergusson said, "Now, listen to me carefully, the two of you. When I give my assent, silently pick up your suitcases and tip-toe to that door." He pointed to a simple white door set in the West Wall of his office. He continued, "Open it as quietly as you can and go through. You will come to a narrow corridor. Walk down it. DO NOT take any turns. Just go straight. After about ten minutes, you two will come to a dead end. But if you two look carefully, you will notice a trapdoor set in the floor. Open it and sneak out. The western frontier will be in front of you. No one from the opposition will notice the two of you there. Climb into the boat that is waiting for you two and sail away. Soon after you reach your destination, you boys will get instructions on what to do next. Now, travel as smartly as you can. Avoid performing any unnecessary tasks and don't plunge headfirst into any trouble, fine? Well, I wish the two of you all the best. Go carefully. And, in case you people encounter any trouble in the boat, there is an S.O.S machine in the main room, the hold as well as in the dormitory. Are there any questions you two want to ask?"

"So, where do we disembark from the boat?" I asked. "Oh, at Marseille," Commander Fergusson answered. I scratched my head [an annoying action I sometimes subject my body to] and asked, "But won't travelling by ship to Marseille be a long-cut?" I questioned. Commander Fergusson sighed and replied, "I am afraid the northern part of France is not the best place to visit in times like these. The southern part is quite safe at the moment, though there *are* minor reports of violence coming from there."

Martin and I nodded. Deep down in my heart, I felt a pang of paranoia. The plan sounded foolproof, but our lives were at stake. What if something went wrong? What if we couldn't reach the boat? What if we...died?

Commander Fergusson was an expert analyser and I saw his skills come into play when he told us, "I know that this is too much of a risk, but it is the best I can arrange. The western frontier is the safest place to take you two out from. My brother went the same way and no harm came to him. Just keep a positive mind and go. Again, I wish you two all the best of luck. Farewell!"

Martin and I pushed back our chairs [I did it extra carefully] and stood up. We collected our suitcases and walked over to the door. Then, Commander Fergusson said, "Er...Lewis, I have realised that I owe you an apology. I apologise for ignoring you and displaying indifference towards you for the past few days. Your words, though spoken in anger, had meaning. I was wrong."

Needless to say, I was stunned. I had no clue of what to say. Finally, after Martin nudged me in the side, I spoke, "That's alright, Commander. I shouldn't have yelled that day. And there's no need to apologise to me."

With a slight twinkle in his eyes, he said, "Oh, but there is! True soldiers never hold grudges, you see. I see that I must practice what I preach." I just had to smile at that. Commander Fergusson grinned back and checked his watch. He said, "Golly, it is time for the two of you to scoot! Old Rory will have my neck on a plate if you lads do not hurry down. Oh, and Rory is your boatman, just so you know. Those blue eyes of his are the keenest I have ever seen on a person, so I picked him for the job. His brain is also in quite the right place. Also, the name of your boat is *Naval Boat 23*."

The two of us nodded. Martin spoke, "Thank you so much for keeping us in here, Commander. I really appreciate it." I had been planning on saying that, so I got quite miffed when he stole my dialogue. "Yes, Commander, me too," I piped up. Commander Fergusson told us that we were more than welcome, but that we should really get going now. So, with one last look at the office, we turned [me on my heel], opened the door and set off down the corridor, me shutting the door softly behind us.

Chapter 11

A Brush with Death

We walked down the corridor, as quiet as mice. I know, reader, that you are expecting me to say that the corridor's ceiling was so low at times that we had to crawl along or that at others the corridor was so narrow that we had to walk with our shoulders parallel to the walls, but fortunately the corridor was quite easy to walk through. After exactly ten minutes, [I *had* to marvel at Commander Fergusson's estimation skills] we reached the dead end. Martin kneeled down and opened the trapdoor. He then picked up his suitcase and went through. I did the same, closing it over me.

We walked for barely half a minute before we saw an opening a few yards away. We walked out and found ourselves on the beach. We were surrounded by coarse sand and craggy rocks. A red and white board nearby read: CORNWALL NAVAL DEFENCE CAMP- WESTERN FRONTIER. The sea was about quarter a mile away from where we were standing. Sure enough, I saw a boat docked to the shore. We started walking towards there, careful not to lose our balance on the rocky ground. All throughout, I was praying in my mind.

We finally reached *Naval Boat* 23. A tough-looking man stepped out and helped us with our suitcases. I assumed that he was Rory. We then climbed aboard; I almost slipped and fell into the saline waters.

Finally, I was in the central room of the boat. It was not large, but big enough to be comfortable in. Two doors led out of it into other parts of the boat. The man held out his hand and introduced, "The name's Rory Hills. I am your captain for the journey. I know your names, don't worry." I shook hands with him. Rory winked and said, "Well, I think we should better set off now!" I nodded.

Rory exited the room. We three were the only ones aboard. After a few minutes, the boat started. Martin immediately turned greener in the face and clutched his stomach. He bit his lower lip. I glared at him and said [rather ordered], "Go and do your business in the loo." Martin somehow managed to nod, staggered to his feet and exited the central room to find a bathroom. I sighed, looking at his retreating back. The boy was impossible.

I walked over to a bench and sat down. Our suitcases were on the racks above. I closed my eyes and rested my head against the top of the armrest of the bench. It was quiet except for the sounds of the sea outside and the ticking of an old clock that was above the bench opposite to me.

Martin stepped in after ten minutes, looking extremely unwell. His hands were literally quaking and his knees were shaking like there was no tomorrow. I presented him with a glare again. He dragged himself to the bench that was opposite to mine and sat down on it so softly that I thought that his behind was made of fragile china. He slowly leaned back so that his back touched the bench, and within a minute, he was snoring like a drunken ragamuffin.

I shook my head at him in disgust. I looked around the room. There was nothing much that I could do in it. So, I decided to explore the boat. I got up, stretched a bit and walked to the door. I turned the knob, but the door didn't open. I turned it once again. Thinking it to be jammed, I pushed against the door. However, it still remained stubbornly shut. I then took a few steps back and lunged at the door. This attempt of mine was unsuccessful as well. Suddenly, I heard some movement at the other door. I ran over to it and turned its knob, but this one didn't open either. A horrible thought entered my brain.

'What if we've been locked in?' I thought; terror suddenly clouding my logical brain. I tugged at my hair to stop from losing my cool. We had been taught that very clearly in safety lessons: Always try to keep calm and cool in dangerous situations; NEVER panic.

I took a deep breath in and yelled, "Rory?!" There was no answer. "RORY, WHERE ARE YOU?" I bellowed. I still got no response. Suddenly, a thought struck me. Commander Fergusson had mentioned Rory's 'blue eyes'. I remembered with a jolt that the person who had taken us aboard had GREEN eyes, not BLUE. I punched the door in frustration. We had been royally fooled.

I then remembered Commander Fergusson saying that there was an S.O.S machine in the central room. In frenzy, I started searching for it. I could have thrown myself off a cliff for not looking if it was there or not. Finally, I found it in a cabinet. It had been hacked to pieces. Swearing angrily, I threw the battered S.O.S machine down. The S.O.S machines in the dormitory and the hold were obviously of no use to us as we were locked inside.

I suddenly heard a sound behind me. I whipped around. Martin had woken up, most probably because of hearing me shout my guts out. He asked me what was going on. I explained everything to him in few words, trying to keep my voice as curt as possible. As soon as he heard what was going on, his eyes turned wide with fear. I ran to him, caught him by the shoulders and said, "Calm down. You cannot afford to panic." He gulped and started banging on a door. I went to the other one and tried to open it. Suddenly, I felt a hand on my shoulder. I turned around, my hands throbbing and sweat breaking out on my forehead. Martin stood in front of me. He said, "Lewis, the clock has stopped."

I looked at him as if he had gone cuckoo and asked sharply, "So, what does that have to do with..." Suddenly, it hit me. The CLOCK had stopped. But the TICKING had not. Before I could stop it, another horrible thought came into my mind. I swept my gaze around the room, desperately trying to find another clock. I looked at Martin and said, "Let's check this thing, now!" We both set to work, looking for another clock that could be producing the sound, because I didn't want the second mortifying idea that had occurred to me to be true. And, after a few moments, I found it. 'It' was not a clock, but something extremely lethal: a time-bomb. It was hidden extremely cleverly in a cabinet. We had only nine minutes and forty-six seconds.

Very carefully, I pulled the bomb out and set it down onto the floor gently. As soon as he saw the bomb, Martin screamed. I wished he hadn't, because I was trying to find a solution to our problem. I knew that I wasn't going to find one. I knew that the two of us were going to die. But still, something inside me told me to think. "Start finding something sharp, quickly! We'll have to cut its wires!" I ordered. Martin nodded and we started searching the room again. We couldn't escape through the portholes because they were too small. The ticking was now louder than ever. I tried not to look at the bomb, but it was impossible. And whenever I looked at it, I felt a fresh wave of paranoia. But more than anything, I felt infuriated; not at Imposter-Rory, or whoever it was that had put the bomb there, but at myself. That queer feeling inside me continued. It was absolutely maddening! I *knew* that I had a better solution with me.

I looked at the timer on the bomb. We had six minutes and a second on our hands. I closed my eyes and thought about the situation we were in as calmly as I could at that moment. Strangely, my thoughts centred on my geography textbook.

I didn't know why, but I kept on thinking about it. Actually, to be more precise, my thoughts were channelled towards a particular lesson in the book- Belgium. Suddenly, with the speed of a lightning bolt, the answer struck me.

I tore my eyes open and commanded Martin shortly, "Come here." He looked at me; his forehead creased, and asked, "Why?" I said angrily, "Just move your bacons! Don't ask any questions!" He obliged. I took another look at the timer. It read: 03.58. I wiped my brow with my sleeve and said, "Now, follow my actions exactly." Praying for luck in my mind, I ripped my travelling cloak off and threw it some distance away. He looked at it, a thoroughly puzzled expression on his face. I yelled furiously, "Do it, will you?" Still looking confused, he took his coat off as well. Then, as quickly as I could with my trembling fingers, I unzipped my trousers. Looking very confused, Martin did the same. I then glanced at Martin for a moment, took a deep breath and let the urine flow.

We did our business in such a way that almost all the parts of the bomb were covered with our excreted liquids. When we were finished, I closed my eyes tightly and crossed my fingers. The ticking stopped. A stopped clock had saved our lives.

Chapter 12

Aye aye, Captain!

I collapsed onto the nearest bench, my head in my hands [we zipped our trousers after defusing the bomb, don't worry]. I couldn't believe it. I couldn't believe that we had just been saved. I couldn't believe that we were still alive. A queer feeling of fright and disbelief mingled with relief ran through me. The air around us was stinking [don't ask me why]. Martin sat beside me and put his arm around me. I didn't push it away.

"Thanks a lot, Lewis. You saved us! I don't know how to repay you," he thanked. I said, my voice slightly muffled due to my hands, "It is fine. Don't mention it."

"But you *saved* us, Lewis. How can I *not* mention it?"

I lifted my face up from my hands. It was clammy and sweaty. I looked at him and said, "Listen, I know that I rescued the both of us from an excruciating death, but just let it rest for a while, fine? Let's just try to get out of here first." Martin nodded slowly and started pacing the room, looking for a possible exit. I too joined him in his search.

However, after half an hour, we were still stuck inside with no means of escape. Also, I was feeling claustrophobic in the stuffy room. Martin went to one of his suitcases and opened it. He extracted a thick fur coat and wrapped it around his right arm. He then went to a porthole and punched it with all his might. Sure enough, it cracked. After boxing it a few more times, the glass of the porthole shattered.

He un-wrapped his coat from his arm, saying, "At least we'll have some ventilation." I nodded and breathed in the salty sea air that came in through the open porthole. My stomach growled [rather roared]; I had not had any breakfast. I checked the time in Commander Fergusson's watch. It was twenty minutes past eleven. Martin seemed to notice my hunger, so he proposed, "Why don't we get ourselves something to eat? There are a few goodies in my suitcase. We can have brunch. I get awfully sick on boat, but I'm famished, so I'm going to eat to my heart's content." I nodded and he started taking out a few cakes for us to eat.

We sat on the bench and began eating, trying to ignore the unpleasant odour emanating from the defused bomb. I said, "We really have to get out of here. There must be *some* way to leave this bloody boat."

Martin swallowed some cake and suddenly sat up straight. "What if he has still left the keys in the locks of the doors?" He asked, his eyes glittering with a manic light. I looked at him with raised eyebrows and asked, irritated, "And how in the world does that help our case?" He stood up and said, excited, "I've read about such situations in many detective stories! I think I know how to get us out of here- if he has still left the keys in the locks, that is." I rolled my eyes at him and said, "Grow up, Martin. Stuff that detectives do can't actually be done. It's all fictitious nonsense. And anyways, what are the chances of the imposter leaving the keys in the locks?" Martin let out the air in his cheeks and retorted, "It's worth a try. You can sit here and mope, if you like. I'm going to see if it works." I was in an 'argue-with-everyone-you-say-a-dicky-bird-to' mood. I stood up and yelled, "At least I don't take sleeping pills!"

Instantly, Martin's face fell. I almost felt sorry for saying what I did, he looked so pitiable. I turned away from him and started scanning the room again. Martin shuffled to one of his suitcases and opened it. He took a newspaper out and walked over to one of the doors. He slid the newspaper under the door, leaving a corner of it on his side. He then took off his belt and jabbed the keyhole with its buckle. He repeated that action five or six times. Suddenly, a big grin broke out on his fair face. He pulled the newspaper to himself from under the door. And, resting on the newspaper was a brass key!

I was...ecstatic. I jumped around and did a wild jig around the room. And, before I could stop myself, I ran to Martin and enveloped him in a rib-crushing, bone-breaking hug worthy of Will. I let go of him after I realised what I was doing. I cleared my throat and said, "Let's get our rears out of here." Martin smiled widely and unlocked the door. And let me say one thing- we would have impressed bulls, the way we rushed out of the room.

We started searching for the dormitory. We found it after trying three or four doors. I kicked the door open and sure enough, sitting on a table, was an S.O.S machine. I sprinted over to it and was about to send an S.O.S message, when Martin caught my hand, preventing me from doing so. When I looked questioningly at him, he pointed to a small sign at the side of the machine. It was the symbol of Hitler.

I straightened up and exclaimed, "Sodding tosh!"

"Where's that Imposter-Rory, by the way?" Martin asked. I smacked my forehead and said, "He didn't want to die, Martin. There was a bomb in the main room, *remember*?"

We then walked to the hold, only to see that the S.O.S machine there belonged to the opposition too. Martin muttered, "The Nazis used their brains, they did. I bet that Imposter-Rory kept these opposition S.O.S machines so that we would send signals using them to the GERMANS, not to the BRITISH, if we survived the bomb!"

"Yes, by Jove, you're right!" I exclaimed, shuddering at the thought of what would have happened had Martin not pointed out that the machine belonged to the Nazis. I held my hand out to him and said, "You just saved us for the second time today. I must say I admire your observation skills." He ran a hand through his hair and grinned modestly. I slapped him on the shoulder and said, "Now, you can very well save us for the third time. Tell me- *how* in the name of *tarnation* are we going to get help?" Martin's grin slid off his face and a lost expression replaced it. I threw my hands up in the air.

Martin leaned against a wall and said, "Well, self help is the best help. We'll have to do something ourselves."

"True," I agreed.

Martin asked, "Do you realise how wrong the whole plan has gone?"

I nodded and stated very bluntly, "So, the two of us are the only ones in a boat that is drifting about on the Atlantic with a defused bomb and a few S.O.S machines belonging to the opposition. You know, it sounds exactly like an adventure novel." Martin dusted the cuffs of his sleeves and said, in an ambitious tone, "When I was small, I always wanted to become a sailor."

I grinned, "Aye aye, Captain!"

Chapter 13
Martin's Story

"Come on! All hands on deck!"

"Aye aye, sir!"

"You always say that, but you never really do anything."

"Aye aye, sir!"

"Two spokes to starboard!"

"Yessir, captain!"

"Oi, starboard means *right*, you dolt, not *left*!"

The two of us were manning the boat. Believe it or not, reader, we were having a lot of fun. Martin decided to imitate a drunk pirate and I almost died laughing. Then, I started singing sea-chants [They were all made by me] in a silly voice. I would like to share one of them with you:

Oh...how I fancy the sea!
It always excites me
With tasty fish
Served to me on a dish
And barrels and barrels of rum
To keep me hooting for a millennium!

I stopped when I could take it no more. I was clutching my sides and literally bellowing with laughter. Martin, meanwhile, had stopped his Oscar-worthy acting and was leaning over the railing of the small deck and vomiting his guts out. After five minutes of throwing out his insides, Martin emerged, green and ashen-faced.

I raised an eyebrow and remarked, "I pity the fish." He looked around himself for something to throw at me, and when he could find nothing satisfactory, he chucked his shoes.

I dodged them expertly and put on a pretend-hurt face. “Hey, your shoes are *dirty*!” I pouted.

He rolled his eyes and said, “I’m going down to drink some water.” I nodded and he went to get some H_2O. [That means water, you airhead! NEVER forget chemistry; don’t mind me, I’m a bit high at the moment ;)]

He returned to the deck after a few minutes. “It’s a good thing I packed a lot of water. I don’t even want to *think* about what would have happened had I not taken any.”

I smiled and teased, “Don’t worry; the sea is always there - water for free, y’know.”

He smacked his forehead and said, “I don’t want to have a barfing bout again. I’m sure my mouth is stinking like the devil right now.”

“Well, then go and wash it. And just so you know, the devil doesn’t stink- he sprays cologne; I’m sure of it.”

“Oh, keep your thoughts to yourself, for the sake of the Lord!”

“Aah...the Lord! He’s another one who does scent. How else do you think he gets those fair, dimple-cheeked angels to surround him at all times?” I asked, snickering. He rolled his eyes at me.

“Hey, don’t roll those smoky balls of yours at me, they’ll fall out of their sockets one of these days,’ I said in a ‘you-shouldn’t-do-that-it’s-very-bad’ voice.

“And you really shouldn’t mess with that musical voice of yours, it’ll become hoarse,” he retorted, his tone literally dripping with sarcasm.

“Hark who’s talking! You speak as if your voice isn’t hoarse already.”

He turned away from me, muttering something about ‘over-smart gits’. I smiled cockily and went to the railing.

It was a magnificent evening. The horizon was pinkish-orange due to the rays of the setting sun. The eastern sky had already started darkening and stars had begun coming out. Seagulls and birds were flying freely in the twilight sky. The sea was mellow and currents lapped gently against the boat.

However, I could see no sign of land anywhere. I sighed and drummed my fingers on the railing. The two of us didn't even have an inkling of an idea where we were. I was sure of the fact that we were on the Atlantic Ocean, but where *exactly*, I didn't have the foggiest.

'What if we turn up at a place we don't know the language of?' I thought to myself. [I was following Martin's advice; don't worry, I'm still high] 'That'll be quite the Robinson Cruiso situation, won't it?' I laughed and rubbed my hand over my cheeks. Cool sea breezes blew, causing my brown waves to fly like some sort of hyperactive burnt noodles.

Martin appeared by my side. "Nice weather, don't you think?" He asked. I nodded in reply. Suddenly, I turned and questioned, "Why did you take so many pills, Martin?"

He sighed and ran a hand through his red hair, messing it up. His blue eyes held a certain poignant look in them that I cannot quite place. He breathed in deeply and answered, "My whole family died a few weeks ago. The whole affair was hushed up terribly. They were all murdered."

I was stunned. I stared at the currents in the ocean, trying to imagine the things Martin had just told me. He continued, "The police are on the case. I'm sure the person-or persons-who killed my parents, will be caught soon; that is, if they haven't been caught already. I escaped because I was out of town with my grandmother. My family meant a lot to me and still does so, Lewis. Obviously, when I heard the news of its death, I got the shock of my life. I couldn't bear to stay home. I couldn't stomach seeing anyone. So, I gathered up all my belongings and started staying at an inn. One evening, very much like this one, I was walking back to Clark's Inn. I had taken a shortcut, so I was walking across the ground that is behind the inn. Suddenly, I heard a lot of loud and rowdy noises coming from behind a few trees. Curiosity entering my brain, I went to investigate. I saw a group of three boys who looked a bit older than me. They asked me who I was and why I looked so sad. And, oh Lewis! I told them that my family had died and I was left all alone. I know I shouldn't have, but I thought I felt an aura of 'kind brotherliness' around them. They sympathized with me and told me that everything would be fine. One of them offered me a tablet and asked me to have it. He called it a pacifier- but it was a pain tablet, though I did not know that at that time. I put it inside my mouth, and that, Lewis, is the biggest mistake I ever made in my entire life. The moment the pill touched my tongue, I felt my head getting lighter. The world became slightly blurred. My breath came out hot and ragged. The boys put another one into my mouth. My head began aching badly and I fell down onto the hard ground of the common. I was feeling terrible. They stuffed more tablets inside my mouth, and ran away! I was left on the ground, writhing and trembling. The whole experience was awful. But, that was not the worst part." He stopped and rubbed his temples. I put my hand on his shoulder and squeezed it consolingly. He gave me a sad look and resumed, "The worst part was that, even though it was so horrible, I loved it. And I wanted more. I somehow managed to stand up with the support of an oak tree. I felt like an absolute zombie. I moved about, searching for those lads, but they were nowhere to be seen. I was hungry for more. I wanted those pills. Just by handing me a few tablets, those boys shattered me. They had made me an addict.

"Somewhere, at the back of my brain, I heard a voice yelling at me to get to the inn immediately and tell someone about what had happened. But I did not want to share the fact that I had become what I had become with anyone. Finally, I gathered my strength and started walking towards the inn. And then, on the way, I met you. I felt like telling you everything, but I just could not. I tossed and turned in bed that night, craving for more. Frustration coursed through my being. In my anger, I tore one of my bed-sheets to scraps and stuffed it hard into my cupboard. The next day, I went to the down-market and bought bottles and bottles of those pills. I rushed to my room and started consuming them. I felt very dizzy. And before I could do anything about it, I fell into unconsciousness.

"I woke up in a hospital room, surrounded by doctors. They helped me get rid of most of my addiction. But I have not been cured fully. Sometimes, I have a deep desire to have those pills again. Dr. Carter told me very strictly to stay away from pills, drugs, alcohol and tobacco, because, you know..."

His voice trailed off. He stared at the dusky horizon. I looked down at my feet and up at him again. I thought I saw tears welling up in his eyes. "Hey, Martin," I said, "I'm sorry for yelling at you. It wasn't your fault that you became an addict. Please forgive me." He looked at me and smiled sadly. He said, "That's fine, Lewis. You didn't know at that time."

I put my arm around him and patted his back. Suddenly, he turned to face me and took my shoulders in his hands. Fierce emotion was burning in his eyes. He said furiously, "Lewis, DO NOT TOUCH PILLS OR DRUGS OR ANYTHING THAT WILL ADDICT YOU TO IT IN YOUR LIFE. Trust me, they may seem 'top' to you now, but later, when you have had a dose, you will get to know what sort of torture on the body these things are. Heed my words today, Lewis, and save your future tomorrow. I don't know why pain pills were invented, but I as sure as hell know one thing- they are EVIL."

His turquoise eyes seemed to pierce through mine. I gulped and nodded. His intense gaze softened. He let go of my shoulders and looked at the horizon. "We can't go on like this forever," I said, changing the topic. "I expect the boat's fuel will come to a zero in a few days and so will our food. We should stick to rations."

"I know," Martin said. "By the way, that was very clever of you- thinking up a way to defuse the bomb. You thought about the Manneken Pis, right?"

I grinned back modestly as my thoughts wandered over to the statue of the boy who had saved a load of people from a bomb blast by urinating on the spot where the bomb had been placed, purely by co-incidence.

"Thank you, pal. And it was quite remarkable of you to get us out of that room alive."

He waved my compliment off. Suddenly, a thought occurred to me [yes, yes, I know. That happens to me a lot]. I looked at Martin and asked, "Martin, why did you change your name?"

He replied drily, "I obviously couldn't have anyone recognising me."

Suddenly, with a jolt, I realised that his father was dead and he was his father's heir...

I winked, "Shall this lowly slave get you the six-tiered rich chocolate and vanilla cake or the exotic Arabian turkey and lamb with sautéed peppers, Your Dukeness?"

P.S: The credit for the creation of the last word goes only and, I repeat, *only* to me.

Chapter 14

A Pleasant Surprise

I woke up early the next day. I had dozed off in the dormitory [I know it was not wise for both of us to doss like that, but what could we have done? Human beings *do* get fatigued!]. The beds there were comfortable and the blankets made me feel as snug as a bug in a rug. Martin was deep asleep, snoring gently.

Feeling mischievous, I decided to wake him up in a less-than-gentle manner. I yelled something along the lines of 'Hail Christ, here I come!' and rugby-tackled him. He woke up with a yell and tried to shake me off. I pressed my knees against his sides and began tickling him.

"Lewis, please GET OFF ME!" Martin bellowed.

I laughed and continued to tickle him. He gasped for breath and yelled, "I beg you! For heaven's sake, please stop tickling me!" Finally, I got off his bed. He heaved a sigh of relief and sat up. He ran a hand through his red hair, making it messier than ever.

I smirked and asked, "What; are you trying to give that Barnet Fair of yours the 'Hunk of Heartbreak' look or summat?"

He smiled and replied, "I don't need to give myself that, I already *am* a hunk of heartbreak."

"More like a skunk of lunch-break," I sniggered. He rolled his eyes and gave me a go-and-fry-your-face look. I stuck my tongue out at him like a silly three-year-old and left the dormitory for the central room.

Days passed quickly. We kept on sailing and looking for land. However, our rations of food and water were depleting fast and I knew that they would finish off completely if we did not get to land as fast as possible. However, good luck was soon going to come to us.

I was awakened at precisely 7.21 am by the sun rays that streamed through the window beside my bed falling on my face. Martin was still slumbering [what a prize sleepy-head!]. I decided not to wake him up this time and step out onto the deck instead.

The weather was rather cool, and I shivered slightly, hugging my arms around myself. The deck was wet. Evidently, it had rained during the night. I walked to the railing and tried to squint through the fog to catch sight of land, but it was so thick that I couldn't see beyond a few yards from the ship.

Pessimistic thoughts ran through my mind. Horrid scenes of us dying on sea floated around in my brain. I shook my head to rid it of them. 'Think positive!' I fiercely told myself again and again, remembering what Will had told me that day at the Cornwall Naval Defence Camp.

I lit the fog lamps on the sides of *Naval Boat* 23, and hoping to the Lord that our boat wouldn't get sliced by a massive ocean liner, I turned to go back inside and change my clothes. And of course, on the way back, I *had* to slip and fall painfully on my rear. With the support of a nearby wall, I got up, only to land on the deck again. Cursing the water on the deck, I pulled myself off the ground and exited the deck carefully so that I would not hurt my poor backside any more.

I found Martin awake and combing his hair when I finally entered the main room [it took me a good twenty minutes]. "So, working on the fur again, Your Dukeness?" I teased. He rolled his eyes [one of his signature moves] and said, "Don't term my hair as '*fur*', Lewis. And please put a lid on calling me 'Your Dukeness'. Believe me, it is really annoying."

"But you *are* the Duke of Leicester, aren't you? Now, can this poor slave do anything for His Excellency?" A second later, I had to duck to save myself from the comb he hurled at me.

"So, did you glimpse any land?" Martin asked, hopefulness shining in his turquoise eyes. I shook my head and replied, "Naw, man. The fog outside's just too thick. But I can always look for it after the fog clears."

Martin's hopeful expression waned, but he replaced it with an 'oh-everything's-okay expression'.

Martin said, "Well, I hope you turned on the fog lamps, then. As for the fog, it can't be any thicker than your skull."

'At least he's not moping around,' I thought to myself. I rolled my eyes laughingly and retorted, "Well, at least my jokes make some sense. And I remembered to light the lamps, thank you very much." He widened his eyes and said, in a voice a four-year-old girl would use to address her favourite doll, "Oh...being the *angry young man*, are we?"

"Well, at least I'm *young*. You look like you've seen more than ninety summers."

Martin opened his mouth to say something, but closed it quickly. He grumbled, "Why do you always have to win?"

"It is probably because I'm better at coming up with repartees?"

"You know something? You may actually be right."

"I *am* right, you dim Duke!"

Breakfast was a simple affair. We had one or two loaves of bread and some canned milk. After we were finished, Martin surveyed the food that was remaining sadly. "We have very little remaining, Lewis. We *have* to spot land."

"I know, chum. And, just so you know, we can skip a meal or two. Don't worry; we'll get to land safe and sound."

"I hope we do," Martin said, staring out of a porthole. "The fog has cleared. I'm going to go and look for you-know-what."

"Well, good luck with that," I said. Martin shrugged, stood up, turned on his heel [the nutcase copied my action] and walked out. I sighed and looked down at my hands, thinking [as positively as I could] about the situation we were in and about ways for us to survive if push came to shove.

All of a sudden, I heard a loud whoop and almost jumped out of my skin in fright. The next second, a very excited Martin rushed inside the room [I wondered how he had made it across the deck so fast without slipping]. I stood up, fearing that something had gone wrong. "Come on, tell me what's wrong!" I exclaimed. He gasped for breath and held up his hand, asking me to wait. It was absolutely unnerving. My patience was about to reach a critical limit. After a few seconds, he said, "I found it, Lewis! I found land!"

Then, the two of us rushed out onto the deck like hooligans that were being chased by the Sweeney [miraculously, I didn't slip!]. Martin ran to the railing on the starboard side, pointed with his index finger and yelled, "Look!" I sprinted next to him and swept my gaze over the water. And at last, I saw it too. Wonderful, fabulous, magnificent land far away! Also, to add to my immense ecstasy, I caught sight of a few vessels here and there. My already huge grin widened and I clapped Martin on the shoulder.

"Race you to the wheel, Your Dukeness!"

Chapter 15
Towards Land

We had finally spotted land, and the two of us were jubilant. However, we were quite far away from it, and had no idea when we would reach the shore. We sailed as fast as we could wangle, determined to get to the land as soon as possible. Also, it was clear to me that Martin was still worried.

"Hey, cheer up, mate. We'll be fine," I comforted him. He said sullenly, "Will we?"

By the end of the day, we were closer. Now, the piece of land became much bigger. I could see other vessels and even a few fishing-boats. I also caught sight of a few hills on the land that we were heading towards. Martin said, "Well, I reckon we have covered considerable distance, then."

"We certainly have, mate," I smiled. "See, what'd I tell you?" He grunted and nodded. Like the one before it, the dusk was simply beautiful. Martin commented. "It's a lovely evening."

"Isn't it?" I asked. He looked at me, whipped around and walked off the deck without saying a single word. I raised my eyebrows and breathed deeply, closing my eyes. Martin, after all, was Martin.

I gripped the railing tightly with my hands and started humming a short hymn my mother had taught me when I was a little child. It is still my most favoured hymn in the entire world. It always gives me a good feeling about everything.

I opened my eyes after I finished the hymn. I cocked my head to one side as I thought about my mother. 'She must be in Spain right now,' I thought. 'I hope to the heavens that she is alright. I can't wait to see her again.' A smile played across my lips as I remembered the moments I had shared with my mother. Reader, my mother has always been my best friend. I love her more than anyone or anything else in the world. I always tell her about everything that happens to me- the good things and the bad. I felt like being with her at that very moment. I felt like hugging her tightly and kissing the top of her head like I always did.

We ate a little bit less than usual for dinner as we had to conserve food. Both of us were silent during our meal. After we finished eating and clearing up, Martin said, "We will have to take shifts to steer *Naval Boat 23 to make sure that we move in the right direction towards the shore*." "Yes, we'll definitely have to," I agreed. He stared down at the floor, brow creased and hands clasped together. "I'll take the first shift," I said. He looked up at me and asked, "Are you all right with it?" He asked. I nodded and glanced at Fergusson's watch. It was 8.40.

"So, we can steer together until it's ten o' clock. Then, you go off to bed and I'll look after the steering. I will come to wake you up at three in the morning. Then, you can take over the steering until eight, fine?"

"Fine; it sounds like a good plan to me." He smiled a small smile at me. I smiled back at him and the two of us went to start steering *Naval Boat 23*.

At precisely ten o' clock, Martin stood up to go off to bed. Before leaving, he gave me a small mariner's compass he had found in a cabinet in the central room to help me navigate. Martin then wished me goodnight and left the deck. I began steering alone. The wheel cabin was situated about ten feet away from the tip of the deck. The walls and the door of it were made of strong glass, so I could see what was going on outside.

The atmosphere was soon enveloped with mist, but it was quite thin, which was a good thing as it allowed me to navigate properly through the saline waters. Time passed, and I continued steering. However, the temperature soon dropped by five or six degrees, and I had to rush inside to fetch a coat for myself.

After about forty minutes, I began hearing great rolls of thunder. A minute later, tiny raindrops started falling onto the deck; and a minute after that, what had started off as a light drizzle turned into a ferocious downpour. Huddling into my coat, I ran outside and lit the fog lamps. Needless to say, I was soaked through when I returned to the confines of the wheel cabin. I shrugged off my coat and, my teeth chattering wildly, I wrung it. I was quite surprised at the amount of water it had absorbed. It was truly raining cats and dogs. Because of the rain and the mist, which had thickened, it was very difficult for me to steer. Finally, I decided to anchor our boat. I rushed out onto the deck for the second time, grabbed the ice-cold anchor and threw it over the port side [left side] of the boat. *Naval Boat 23* stopped sailing after a few moments and I ran back inside the small wheel cabin, but not before heaving a huge sigh of relief.

Once I was inside, I stole a glance at Fergusson's watch. It was 12.15. I wrung my coat again. However, I decided that it was too wet to wear after that, so I went inside to fetch another one. Also, I carried several blankets that I had found in one of the cupboards of the dormitory to keep me warm.

I ran as fast as I could without slipping to the wheel cabin. I entered it and sat down on a chair that was very conveniently nailed to the floor of the deck, wrapping the blankets around me. As soon as I sat down, I had a violent bout of sneezing. 'Darn it, I'll probably have a chill in the morning,' I thought.

The minutes ticked by. There were many times when I was on the verge of sleep, but I pinched and scratched my arms to keep myself from the realms of slumber. The downpour finally gentled into a drizzle. The mist, too, started to become thinner. Finally, at exactly twelve minutes past one, the rain stopped completely and the mist disappeared too. However, the weather was still colder than ever.

I was extremely reluctant to leave the warm cosiness of the blankets, but the prospect of reaching land as soon made me stand and pull up the anchor. I also put out all the fog lamps. I resumed steering with the help of the compass Martin had given me.

Finally, at three o' clock, I left the wheel cabin and went to the dormitory to wake Martin. I left the blankets in the cabin as I knew that he would need them.

It took me a few minutes to wake him up. He sat up with a jerk and sighed in relief when he saw that it was only me who was shaking him and not some minion of hell. I related the events of the night up until then to him in a few words. He grunted and, swinging his long legs over the edge of the bed, stood up. After yawning and stretching for a few seconds, he sauntered off to the deck. I went to the bed that I had slept on the night before that one and dropped off within minutes, without bothering to undress.

I was shaken awake the next morning by an extremely hyperactive Martin. "*Oi*! Leggofmeck [let go of my neck]!" I gasped. Martin pulled my blanket off my person. The blast of air that was icy cold to my skin after the warmth of the blanket made me sit up. I yawned widely and rubbed my eyes. Martin grabbed my shoulders and tried to drag me off my bed. I, not to be outdone, kicked him hard in the stomach. Martin let go of my shoulders, making me fall backwards and bang my head on the bedpost- the kick wasn't such a good move on my part after all.

Martin, who had recovered from my fast-one to his abdomen, said, "Lewis! Get up! We're very close- very close to land!"

Chapter 16
Flu Flew to Me

Martin dragged me by the collar to the deck. He grinned, waiting for my reaction. My jaw plummeted down and my eyes almost fell out of their sockets. "THIS IS BLOODY AMAZING!!!" I yelled. Martin, shaking his head, simply laughed and said, "See; what did I tell you?"

We were very close to land. I could clearly make out trees, houses and cars. There were tons of fishing boats, ships and yachts all around us. I couldn't believe our luck. Everything was just too good to be true!

I opened my mouth to say something, but was cut off by the loud sneeze that escaped my mouth. It was such a violent one that I bent down and staggered slightly. I felt Martin's hand clasp my shoulder to steady me. I stood straight and said, "It certainly looks as if last night's cold weather has victimized me."

Martin nodded, but didn't say anything. He pulled me inside the dormitory despite my vehement protests, made me undress, wear a thick coat on top of my pyjamas and get into bed. "I want to be on deck when we reach land!" I complained, sounding very much like a baby who had just been pinched by his elder sibling. Martin shook his head and said, "You need to rest. Your condition will slide if you go on deck. Please don't get out of bed. Try to sleep. And, do pull a blanket or two over yourself." With that, he turned and walked out of the room, ignoring my curses and groans.

I started shivering again, and my brow showed no signs of stopping to sweat. 'Maybe I should really drop off for half an hour or so,' I thought to myself. I pulled the blankets that were piled at the foot of the bed up to my chin and snuggled deeper into my bed. Perspiration was trickling down my face in little streams. I wiped it off with the left sleeve of my pyjamas and tried to doze off, but it seemed impossible. Each and every cell that my body was [and still is, you twit] composed of seemed to be on fire. A restless feeling grasped me. I turned over and closed my eyes; only to open them again as they burned fiercely when I did so.

'Drat it, I've caught a fever,' I thought, frustrated. 'I'm sure there are no medicines on board- that imposter must have taken all of them. Neither Martin nor I have carried any.' I could feel my body getting warmer still. I sang a lullaby that my dear mother used to sing to me softly to myself, waiting desperately for the gentle hands of slumber to caress my eyes. And finally, after what seemed like hours to me but must have been only a few minutes, I dropped off into a feverish sleep.

I was performing in front of a huge crowd. I had my beloved guitar in my hands and a winning smile on my face. The audience was going wild. People were all clapping, screaming and chanting my name. My smile widened out into a grin. I continued singing and strumming my Gibson [guitar]. *Then, all of a sudden, the audience disappeared. Harsh sounds began ringing in my ears. Huge and flaming cracks ran through the stage. I tried to get off it, but couldn't. Suddenly, everything began shaking...*

My eyes flew open. Sparks were doing what seemed to be an overly energetic waltz in front of my eyes. The world was slightly blurred. I closed my eyes tightly, rubbed them and opened them again. Martin's face came into focus. It was endorsing a worried expression. He put his hands under my shoulders and helped me sit up.

I yawned and asked groggily, "What's happened?" Martin answered, "Well, Lewis, you were sleeping for six hours straight! I came down to wake you because..."

"What the hell! I was asleep for *six hours*?!"

"I'm going to get you some food. You go and sit on that bed." With that, he turned and walked out of the door. I sighed and did as he told.

Martin was back a few minutes later, carrying a tray. On the tray was placed some bread and tinned chicken. With a word of thanks, I accepted the tray from him and began eating. Martin drew up a small stool and sat beside my bed. Suddenly, I realised that the boat wasn't swaying anymore [hey, come on! My chill was making me slow!]. I asked, "Have we dropped anchor?"

Martin replied, "Well, I have a piece of good news. We've reached land and I have docked the boat."

"Wow!" I yelled happily. A millisecond later, however, I descended into a violent coughing fit. Martin looked at me disapprovingly and chided, "You really shouldn't raise your voice so much, Lewis. Your throat's condition will worsen if you do so."

"Hey, at least we've gotten to land!" I said, wiping perspiration off my forehead.

Hearing this made the Duke forget his annoyance. A huge grin broke out on his fair face. His blue eyes sparkled with happiness. I mirrored his gesture. His grin widened and a smug look appeared on his visage. He answered, his grin turning into a smirk, "We are at Marseille." The moment I heard these words, I dropped my tray-food and all-and jumped out of bed. I was absolutely ecstatic.

I ran my hands through my hair [which was quite sweaty and giving out a thoroughly unpleasant pong] and said, "Holy Christ, Martin! Luck is definitely on our side! Why, we are quite on track! Even if the plan had gone flawlessly, we would have been at Marseille! Sonofagun, I can't believe it!" Martin rolled his eyes and stood up. "Sit down," he ordered, pointing at my bed. Martin groaned, "Look, Lewis, I understand your feelings, but you just cannot go around singing and acting like a road ruffian when your health has deteriorated. If you behave like this, you will get sicker. So, for that very reason, I suggest you sit down."

Realising that his words made priceless sense, I laid my head back on my pillow and sighed. "You did a good job of convincing me to stop acting like the hooligan I am," I said. He shrugged and smiled.

Chapter 17

Santa Claus Has Come to Town!

I awoke in the evening to find that my temperature had gone down. But, according to Martin, I needed 'rest'. "Seriously, Martin," I said-when we were bunnying in the dormitory-in a complaining tone. "I mean, I'm grateful to you for taking care of me and everything, but don't you think that you are overdoing the 'just take rest' part a bit?" He crossed his arms across his chest and said in a tone an irate mother would use with her petulant child, "Well, for the record, you are *sick*, Lewis. You can't go about behaving like a right Jumping Jiminy. How many times do I have to explain this to you?" I rolled my eyes, but I knew that I was defeated [well, I really *was* ill, so I couldn't chase him around with my shoes yelling 'Death to ye, ye doggone scoundrel!'].

Suddenly, as if he had just remembered something, Martin slapped his thigh and ran out of the room before I had the chance to say 'cor'. I hummed [April in Paris] and stared up at the ceiling, wondering what had gotten into my friend.

The door swung open a minute later and Martin stepped in, a small bag swinging from his left hand. I looked at it questioningly and turned my gaze onto him. He walked over to my bed and said, "I got these for you when I went out."

"You went out into the town?" I asked. He nodded and said, "I decided to take a little stroll in the picturesque town of Marseille as I was registering our boat in the dock office. And, as I was doing so, I bought these for you."

Thinking that Martin had bought me a small trinket as a 'Get Well Soon' gift, I sat up and smiled, looking at the bag with curious eyes.

Martin inserted his right hand into the bag and pulled its contents out. However, I was in for a shock. The moment I saw what he had pulled out, I gagged. Clasped in his bony hand was a bottle of Dr. Hammond's Pills for Cold, Temperature, Headache, Congestion and Sore Throat.

Now, I have another lesson of life for you, reader: NEVER even TRY to consume those tablets. They are the realms of hell and downright devilish blighters. When you pop them into your unsuspecting mouth, they taste all nice and sweet. But, a mere second later, they show their true colours. Their sugary facade dissolves and a terrible bitter flavour spreads in your poor mouth, tormenting your tongue. It is an utter torture [well, they do cure you, but that is quite beside the point!]. Martin brandished the wicked things at me and ordered, "You have to take one of these every night for three days." I covered my mouth with my hand and shook my head vigorously. Martin shook his head and said, "Oh come on, Lewis. You do want to get better, don't you?"

Well, I finally took one of the damned pills, but not before boxing Martin's ears several times. It took up all of my self-control to refrain from being sick all over my sheets and pyjamas. I had to drink up several glasses of water to lessen the nasty taste in my mouth.

"Now, get to sleep. These tablets will speed up your recovery. You should be up and about in no time," Martin asserted as he helped me lie down. I was hit by a tidal wave of sleepiness as soon as my head touched my fluffy pillow. I yawned widely and turned onto my right side, descending into slumber.

My days were brilliant and happy although we could not yet leave the boat due to my condition, but my nights were terrible.

First of all, I had to take those horrid tablets before sleeping. Secondly, nightmares began invading my sleep. In one of them, I saw a fierce war raging. Soldiers were being killed left, right and centre. And, in the midst of it all stood Lord Ares, two massive hounds encircling him.

In the second one, I saw El Diablo himself- Adolf Hitler. In this nightmare, Hitler was standing on a raised platform situated in a simply massive hall in front of hundreds of German soldiers. A large banner with the Nazi Swastika on it was behind him. He was wearing a German military suit and yelling at his soldiers in German. I have learnt German in school, so I understood what he was saying- "Go, my Nazis! Go and fight courageously for all that you are worth! Fight until the last breath in your body leaves you! Do this, my faithful men, and we can conquer the world. Those English rats are nothing in front of us. Perform your best, men, and victory will surely be ours!" Mad cheering and hooting emanated from the soldiers. They raised their weapons said, [in German, of course] "For the Nazis!"

In the third nightmare, I saw myself. Only, I was much younger in it; around five years old. I was standing outside a wooden door, my ear fixed firmly to it. I could hear the muffled voice of a man inside. "...the papers are in the second drawer. They explain all about what will..."

Suddenly, a light breeze blew. It caused a few loose specks of dust on the door to enter my nose. The very next second, I sneezed loudly.

The man suddenly stopped talking and asked sharply, "Who's there?" I was paralysed with fear. I heard hurried footsteps coming towards the door. I turned tail and ran, terrified. However, I was in such a hurry that I tripped over my feet and fell straight onto an upturned rusted nail. Tears streaming out of my grey eyes, I cried out in pain for help.

The funny thing was that I couldn't, for the life of me, remember when I had gotten injured like that. Also, my mother would have surely taken me to the hospital immediately if something like that had happened to me. I racked my brain but I couldn't recollect being in a hospital when I was around the age of five. And, that nail was quite sharp. It would have left behind a wound in my abdomen. And I assure you, reader, I have no such thing.

In the fourth and final nightmare, I saw Will. But, the cheerful smile that his face was usually adorned with was absent. His eyes were glinting with a strange manic light. His jaw was set. In his right hand was a lethal-looking rifle. In front of him was a crying woman.

The woman was wearing a red and blue robe that was trimmed with white. She was very beautiful, but her lovely features were marred by the tears flowing down her face. Her hands were clasped together. She screamed, "How can you do this to me? I am your mother!"

The next second, he raised the rifle and cocked it. I yelled at him to lower it, but he paid no heed to me [of course he paid no heed to me! It was all a nightmare, wasn't it?]. The next second, he pulled the trigger, very much to my horror.

The bullet hit his mother's arm. She shrieked in agony as blood poured out of the wound. I tried to run to Will and wrest the rifle from him, but my legs felt like lead. I couldn't move. Will shot her again and again. A pool of blood formed around her.

Mrs. Fergusson wailed, wept and bawled for mercy, but her pleas fell on deaf ears. She was seriously wounded.

I kept yelling at Will to stop shooting at her. Suddenly, she gasped loudly. I turned around to face Will's mother and tried to sprint towards her, but I couldn't move an inch. "Damn it!" I roared angrily. Mrs. Fergusson slumped to the ground a second later, completely devoid of life.

I wondered what these horrible dreams could possibly mean. I knew that the first one was telling me about the impending war, but the others sort of scared me. The one which alarmed me the most was the one in which Will was shooting his own mother. If there's one thing I hate, it's witnessing something bad happening and not being able to do anything about it. Even now, it drives me nuts.

Also, Will looked quite dangerous in that dream. However, the thing that astonished me the most was the fact that Will was actually *harming* his mother [I told you, I would die for Mater]. Martin kept asking me about my dreams, but I always answered him with the same blunt 'No.'. But I had to admit to myself, they bothered me.

'They're just stupid nightmares,' I thought fiercely. 'They can never become reality. So stop worrying so much about them!' But I still didn't completely get over them.

After a week by the Marseille docks, my condition became totally positive. My fever had disappeared and so had my cold.

That night, as the two of us were having the bread and cheese that Martin had bought from the marketplace near the docks, Martin said, "Lewis, you are in perfect shape now. I'm very happy for you." I grinned and said, "It's great to be healthy again. And, as much as I hate to admit it, those infernal pills helped."

"We are leaving *Naval Boat 23...*" he said. Realisation dawned upon my face. I grinned, "So, Skipper, when do we abandon ship?"

I was a bit sad to leave our boat. We had almost been killed aboard it, but you know, certain things tend to start growing on me.

It was a bright day. The sky was a beautiful cerulean. A few small, wispy clouds interspersed it. Aves chirped happily as they flew above the Marseille docks. I smiled as we walked into them. We hurried over to a small bench that was a few yards away from us and placed our suitcases down onto it.

Martin said, "We'll have to take up jobs, you know. We have only about eleven pounds left. I suppose we *will* have to work."

I smirked, "We can always rob a bank." Martin smacked the back of my head and said, "We are not going to do anything of the sort."

I raised my arms in surrender and said, "Hey, hey, I was only joking!" [I was going to add 'Your Dukeness' after 'joking', but I wisely refrained from doing that. Christ knows what he would have done to me had I allowed my tongue to run free]

Martin continued, "Then, when we have enough money, we can head towards Geneva." I nodded and said, "We can work at the docks. But, we also need a place to stay."

"Is not the answer to the lodging problem obvious? We are going to stay at an inn," Martin suggested. I groaned, "I've just about had *enough* of inns." Martin shook his head and picked his luggage up, I followed suit. He then grabbed my hand and, dragging me along, said, "Oh, just shut up and come along, will you? We can't hover around here forever."

For a person who had just recovered from overdose, Martin had amazing muscular power. He dragged me along as if I was a feather, not a teenage youth of fifty kilograms.

And, he was also carrying his suitcase. Meanwhile, I was struggling with my own.

Reader, if you have not already been there, let me describe Marseille to you. It is a busy little town; a typical French one. The people there are kind and ready to help. The place is very neat and tidy. The roads there are nice and wide and the houses are simple yet charming.

Martin asked around a bit and we soon found a good inn [I made a face] a quarter mile away from the docks. It was smaller than Clark's Inn, but, looked like a nice place. We gave fake names to the receptionist, of course. I christened myself Linton Holmes [I took 'Linton' from Wuthering Heights- my mother's favourite book. Now, I haven't read the piece of work, but my mother has told me the names of all the characters in it and I have to say, I thought the name 'Linton' was quite 'top'. (I know that I have told you that I am good at English, but Wuthering Heights is for *girls*. You can't really blame me for not reading it.) And of course, I took 'Holmes' from Sir Doyle's classic series. Also, Holmes happens to be my mother's maiden surname] and Martin posed as a certain Robert Finley.

The room we got was a cosy one. It was on the second floor and, of course, as clean as a whistle. It had a lovely view of the town. There were two beds inside it, a large wardrobe, a table and an armchair. A door beside the wardrobe led to the bathroom, which was painted a pleasant blue colour that reminded me of the sea. A thick white carpet covered the floor.

As soon as we stepped inside, Martin literally bolted and snagged himself a bed. I rolled my eyes [well, Martin copied my action, so give me one reason why I shouldn't have copied his, yo!] and went over to the other bed. I slipped my coat off, removed my shoes and socks and lay back on the bed. It was very comfortable. I smiled contentedly and closed my eyes.

Suddenly, I realised something and sat up. I turned to look at Martin and said, "We've been very stupid."

He faced me and asked, "Why do you say that?"

"Well, we came in a naval boat belonging to England. Also, the dock folks are sure to search it when they run their security checks. They'll sure as hell find that bomb. We'll be taken to the Sweeney and our true identities will be revealed."

Martin simply rolled his eyes [I felt like whipping him. Seriously, his eye-rolling move had started to annoy me]. "I'm sure the authorities have been informed about us. This is Europe, Lewis. Things spread like wildfire through the agencies. Also, that bomb is now defused. It's not going to harm anyone," he said.

But I was still not convinced. "But what if they don't know about us? We could be put behind bars or worse, caught by Hitler's men!" Martin rolled his eyes [urgh!] and said, "You worry too much. If you had looked around properly, you cock-eyed bozo, you would have noticed something. I have painted over the name of the boat with some paint that I found in the hold and called it something else - Aurelie Renoir. It is a tight French name. Also, Commander Fergusson was very clever to send us in a boat that looks just like French fishing one. I'm sure Hitler's men won't have a clue. Also, my father..." He faltered, a sad expression creeping onto his handsome face.

I said, "I understand your sadness, mate. But be happy that you at least had a father who sodding *loved* you. Mine treated me like a sick pouch."

Martin laughed weakly and said, "Well, anyway, my father, as he was the Duke of Leicester, knew how fast everything goes. During the Great War, messages were passed from country to country with the speed of lightning. And I'm sure their speed has not lessened at all. You worry a lot, do you know that? Hey, don't look at me like that! Worrying only causes you to get more and more tensed. I'm telling you right now what you told me on the boat- STAY POSITIVE."

"But this is not a question of staying positive, Martin! I'm worrying because I *care*!"

"If you care, that's good enough. Why do you need to worry on top of that? Worrying simply strains your nerves. Just sitting and making a royal fuss will *never* help."

I groaned and said, "I'm going for a bath."

Well, reader, I have something to tell you. Whenever you step out of the bathroom wrapped in a towel, ALWAYS make sure that the towel is tight enough. This should give you a good idea of what happened when I stepped out of the loo.

I exited the bathroom, closing the door behind me, a towel wrapped around my middle. And, as soon as I took a step towards my suitcase, the wretched item fell straight down; leaving me arse-starker in a room that had its windows wide open. And of course, Martin was there too to roar with laughter at me.

Now, one of the many things that I cannot tolerate is someone laughing at me. So, I didn't feel sorry in the slightest when I ran straight to him and smacked his stupid face. And let me tell you, his laughter ceased immediately after that.

"Ouch, Lewis," Martin groaned, rubbing his cheek, which had now turned a violent shade of red. "You shouldn't have laughed at me if you didn't want my hand to leave a little present on that countenance of yours." Martin muttered, "I apologise, Lewis. I shouldn't have done that." I grunted and began shutting all the windows in the room. Then, I put on my clothes.

Silence enveloped us. It was broken a few minutes later by Martin. "It's almost time for lunch. Do you want to go down for a bit of food? I can take a bath after lunch." I readily agreed. He flashed me the 'all's well' sign.

I turned [on my heel] and walked over to the door, Martin following right behind. I put my hand on the doorknob and twisted it to the right.

As soon as I opened the door, I got the shock of my life. I gasped loudly, my eyes wide. Standing in front of me, with a wide grin on his freckled face, was none other than Will!

His grin widened when he saw my expression. I spluttered, astounded, "W-Will?! How the hell did you..."

He winked and said, "Santa Claus has come to town!"

Chapter 18

At the Restaurant

Martin looked on, an amused expression on his face, as I grabbed the scruff of Will's neck and pulled him inside our room, shutting the door with my right foot. I roughly dragged him to Martin's bed and sat him down. "Ow!" Will yelled in pain. "You just broke my rear!" I squared my shoulders and roared, "I thought you were supposed to be in Zurich. What the bloody hell are you doing here?" Martin looked at me, a scandalised expression on his face, and said in a chiding voice, "Lower your voice, you gewgaw! We're not supposed to be revealing anything about us to anyone, *remember*? I'm afraid that won't happen if you yell to the skies and speak!"

Will breathed in deeply and said, "Hey, gimme two shakes to catch my breath, will you?" I glared at the hazel-eyed male. And, as I did so, my nightmare about him suddenly resurfaced. 'Shut up!' I told my mind. 'It's just an idiotic nocturnal vision! Stop being such a prat about it!'

Finally, Will looked up and explained, in a low voice "Well, I received a line a few days ago from Asher Cox [when he said the name, his eyes flitted around the room to make sure that all the windows were closed] telling me to stay in Geneva. I was also told the name of the inn I was to stay in."

I narrowed my eyes and asked, "How did this Asher Cox communicate with you at a time like this? Who is he, anyway?" Will's gaze swept over the room once more before he answered, "My brother writes telegrams under the name 'Asher Cox'. He used the SSCSB- the Secret Speedy Communication Service of Britain. I got the letter from a British secret outlet here in Marseille." I nodded in understanding.

Martin questioned, "Do you have any idea why he asked you to stay here?" Will nodded and replied, "Yes, I do. First of all, my brother wanted the two of you to catch up with me. I don't think he trusts me to travel alone." I didn't say anything out loud, but I agreed with Commander Fergusson wholeheartedly. Will could be very goofy at times.

"Secondly," Will continued, "The train I was supposed to be catching here at Marseille got caught in an accident, and it's damaged rather badly. Of course, I could've caught another one, but it seems that Hitler had a hand in the accident. My elder one didn't want me to take any risks, so...well, I guess I'm y're travel mate now!"

"Well, I'm happy to see you, Will," Martin said, extending his hand. Will shook it and looked at me. I shrugged and said, "Hey, I just got a bit paranoid seeing you like that." Will shook his head in mock-disgust and said, "I'm rather hungry. We should really lay our hands on some lunch, don't you chappies think?"

"Well, that's where the two of us were headed off to, before you turned up out of the blue," I said. Will smirked and the three of us exited the room, Martin adjusting the buttons on the left cuff of his coat.

The dining room was medium-sized. Fifteen to twenty tables dotted it. The floor was covered with a fluffy carpet that was quite similar to the one in our room. The walls light yellow and the ceiling was a pleasant off-white hue. Waitresses attired in sky blue dresses served huge loaves of bread, stew and a few other weird French foodstuffs.

Will spotted an empty table in a corner and the three of us trudged over to it and sat down- Martin and I on one side and Will on the other. A menu-card was placed on the table. The three of us reached for it at the same time and, of course, a hand-fight *had* to happen.

So, after quite a few pinches, scratches and pokes, Will emerged successful. He stuck his tongue out at us like a git and began reading the menu-card, holding it annoyingly out of our reaches, so we couldn't even grasp it from him. After ten excruciating minutes, he handed it over to the two of us. Martin held the menu-card while I looked at it over his shoulder. Like the Candling I am, I focused on the prices of the items rather than the items themselves. [I suppose I must tell you this: The three of us were blind enough to miss the fact that a waitress had kindly laid two more menu-cards on our table. Seriously! We didn't notice them until we were about to leave the dining room]

Martin looked at me and asked, "What would you like to have, Lewis?" "Oh, anything that costs below seventy-five pence. Make sure it has no carrots too," was my reply. Will rolled made a face at me.

A waitress [the same one, we later found out, who kept the two menu-cards on the table] came over to us and asked, "Please may I take your order, Monsieurs?" Martin nodded and ordered some salad that had a weird name, fondue and something else that [Martin told me later] contained halibut in it [I don't know a word of French. They taught German at my school].

Will drummed his fingers on the table and looked around, a bored look in his hazel eyes. Suddenly, he straightened up as if he had just remembered something important. "I need to pay a visit to the loo," he mumbled. He pushed back his chair, conveniently tipping it over, and, without bothering to offer the poor chair a second glance, literally strutted out of the dining room.

"What's bitten *him*?" Martin asked me, his face sporting an expression of confusion. I shrugged and answered, "Oh, I haven't the slightest; the Mosquito of Insanity, maybe, your Dukeness has some ideas?" Martin rolled his eyes and chided, "How many times do I have to tell you to stop addressing me as that?" I shrugged. Martin sighed, "Anyway, don't call me that in front of Will."

"Why not?" I asked, surprised.

"Just...don't."

"All right," I agreed. I didn't want to press the topic. "But you have to tell me why later."

Martin smiled and said, "Yes, I will. By the way, don't you think we should pick that chair up and put it right? Someone may trip over it," I looked at him as if he had taken leave of his senses and said, "Well, it's not our fault it fell."

Martin laughed again, just as our food arrived with the same dimply waitress who had taken our order [and you-know-what]. Unfortunately, she did not see the fallen chair. She fantastically tripped over it, causing our trays to go flying. The poor waitress fell flat on her face with a scream. Our food spilled spectacularly all over two men who looked like they were from the early 1870's. The others in the dining room turned to look in our direction.

At that moment, Will entered the room, his hands in his pockets. He was whistling merrily and seemed totally oblivious to what had just happened. And, before anyone could warn him, he tripped awesomely over the waitress, somersaulted not-so-gracefully in the air and banged his behind on the floor. I had a tough time trying to control my laughter and apparently, so did the other people in the room.

Will glared at me, and if looks could kill, reader, I would have been six feet under now, not writing this. Martin, like a perfect gentleman, quickly helped the two of them up. A few other guests of the inn hurried towards us, graciously picked up the fallen trays and kept them on the table. Meanwhile, Martin went and apologized to the two men over whom our food had been spilled. But, he, like a prize fool, forgot to straighten the fallen chair!

Martin shouted as he tripped backwards over the stupid chair and landed right on another waitress, who squealed in agony. I shook my head, stood up, set the chair right and helped my redhead friend and the French waitress up. The latter launched into a tirade of curses. Fortunately for me, I couldn't understand a word of what she was saying. Martin turned and presented Will with one of his glares. His turquoise eyes clearly said: CONSIDER YOURSELF DEAD. Will smiled sheepishly and ran a hand through his ebony hair, saying, "Anyone hungry?"

The moment we reached our room, [Will came into it with us] Martin pummelled Will hard in the gut. Will returned the blow with a hard kick which hit Martin right in the left kidney. I rolled my eyes as the two of them began bickering. Unfortunately, my attempts to make them stop quarrelling all went in vain [The worst part was that I couldn't yell to make them stop. The reason for that is as obvious as the nose on your face].

Finally, after fifteen heated minutes, the two of them stopped their nonsense. I breathed in deeply, sat down on my bed and voiced something that had been nagging my brain for some time, "Will, did you *really* go to the loo when you excused yourself?"

Will answered, "I was about to tell you about that when we entered the room, but this half-brained dweeb punched me before I could get even a single dicky-bird out. I won't be surprised if something's happened to my gut." Martin opened his mouth, no doubt to say something offensive to Will, but I cut him off, "Please tell us everything, Will."

Will plopped down onto my bed beside me and placed his legs on Martin's bed, ignoring the redhead's scowls. He fished a telegram out of his pocket, unfolded it and began to read it aloud.

Chapter 19
To Unit A

"Meet at Unit A at two pm STOP" Will finished with a flick of his hand. "What is 'Unit A'?" Martin asked. Will stood up and answered, "Wait and see." "Well, how are we going to reach there?" I demanded. He replied, as if it was the most obvious thing in the world, "We go by foot, of course."

Martin glanced at his watch and said, "It is one-twenty right now."

Will exclaimed, "Omigosh! We better get marching!" He turned and went straightaway to the door, without bothering to put a coat on. Martin and I looked at each other with our eyebrows raised. "Hey, move your bacons, the pair of you! We can't rabbit the whole damn day!" Will said furiously.

"Do we take our bags with us?" asked Martin. Will shook his head. "They'll be taken care of," he said. Martin and I pulled on our coats and the three of us walked down to the reception.

We gave our room keys to the kind-faced receptionist. We were just about to turn and leave the building, when the receptionist said, "Monsieurs, the weather report has said that it is going to rain heavily tonight. The streets will most probably be choked up. Such rains can be very nasty. So, Monsieurs, please try to reach the inn within an hour." We nodded and Martin said [just to go with her flow], "Thank you, madam. We will most certainly be back within sixty minutes!" She smiled at us and the three of us walked out.

The moment we exited the inn, Will repeated the words the receptionist had uttered, in an extremely shrill and mocking tone.

"Shhh! Be quiet, Will," Martin warned. "She may hear you."

"Oh, try not to be so ridiculous, chicky-baby, the door's closed. I bet my buttock those delicate ears of hers haven't caught a single word of our conversation," Will retorted.

"Don't be so sure, old chap. I've heard that the French have sharp ears" I teased,

"Well then, let it be. Let her hear how she is. Maybe she'll become less annoying then."

"I've also heard that the French are obsessed with revenge, so don't come crying to us if you wake up suddenly to find a fierce receptionist standing beside your bed."

"You forgot to mention the butcher's knife she most probably will be brandishing, Lewis."

"Ha ha ha."

"Sod off."

"Oh, piddle someplace else."

"Ehm...boys? It's getting rather late. And that receptionist was right, Will. Those clouds *are* looking quite ferocious."

Will turned to his right and began walking, his hands shoved inside the pockets of his trousers. Martin and I followed him. I couldn't help but notice that the people around us looked rather scared [I know I was being stupid, don't look at me like that. Of course they were scared! Won't you be afraid if you are presented with the prospect of a war?!]

I also saw that the people out on the roads were mostly men - very few women and children could be seen. I also saw plenty of posters stuck on walls of houses and lamp-posts.

They all showed the picture of a rather fierce looking man with a moustache. His face would have been a sight to laugh at had his eyes not been blazing with fury. "Herr Hitler," Martin whispered beside me.

Will continued to walk on. His shoulders were tensed and his pockets were slightly bulged- his hands were evidently balled into fists. I could tell that the very sight of the German psychopath caused his anger to flare.

Gloomy winds blew, making the leaves on trees rustle. I could hear distant rolls of thunder. "It's going to rain cats and dogs," I said "That receptionist was right." I heard Will snort.

On and on and on we moved. I called, "Hey, Will!" He turned around. "How long will we have to walk? It looks like it's going to rain badly." I said. "A few minutes more, and have patience. We will be there before you know it." Will responded. Will let out a gasp and broke into a sprint. Martin and I ran behind him. Will was a fabulous athlete. He ran easily and fluidly. I was panting hard and I could tell that Martin was going through hell. He had clearly never exercised his legs so much before. Finally, after turning a corner Will slowed down to a canter. He looked over his shoulder and said, "We're almost there." I heaved a sigh of relief and wiped my brow with the sleeve of my coat. Martin looked ready to drop dead.

Finally, Will stopped right in front of a small cottage and gestured to us to do the same.

The cottage looked like the sort in which grandmas reside. It was painted a bright pink with white around the windows, so it looked like a strawberry bon-bon with marshmallows. Ivy and honeysuckle grew on the walls. The garden was very well kept. The hedges were neatly trimmed and the flower beds were growing quite nicely.

Will went to the door and opened it. He turned and said, "Come on, you two. We're at Unit A." Martin and I followed him inside.

The interior of the cottage was painted in vibrant shades of purple, orange and hot pink. It was awfully cramped. We were standing in a room that served as a living room, bedroom and kitchen all at once. Two sofa-chairs were pressed against a wall, with a small wooden table in front of them. Beside them was a wardrobe that scraped the ceiling of the room. There was a small bed in the middle. Pillows, cushions and packets of jelly babies were scattered all over it.

There was a kitchen counter to the left. A [pink coloured] clock ticked away above it [immediately, the bomb incident in *Naval Boat 23* came into my mind]. Posters of French, British and American models and actresses lined the walls. The biggest one in the room belonged to Katharine Hepburn [I do not deny the fact that I drooled quite a bit]. I could see stacks of old magazines under the bed. I bent down and tried to pick one of them up and take a look at it, but Will caught my wrist and gestured to me to not do that.

Suddenly, we heard footsteps coming towards the room. It took me half a minute to realise that they were sounding from under the floor of the room. Will whispered, "It's him!" Before I had time to figure out who the person Will had referred to was, the bed suddenly moved towards us and we were all thrown off our feet.

We banged hard against a wall [I, much to my luck, hit the poster of good old Kathy Hep]. I slid to the ground, rubbing my head. It was aching terribly due to the impact with the wall [and the poster, don't forget]. Sparks danced in front of my eyes. I blinked them away, and was quite astonished with what I saw. The magazines under the bed weren't magazines at all. They were part of a trapdoor.

A man climbed out of it, cracking his knuckles and stretching his arms. The moment he saw us, a wide smile spread across his angular face and he said, "So *there* you brats are! I certainly didn't expect you three to be so punctual."

Chapter 20
The McCartney Family

The man who had come out of the trapdoor was tall, broad-shouldered and heavily built. His hair was cut very short, and so were his nails. He was dressed in a bright red suit. He nodded shortly in Will's direction before saying, in a thick Liverpudlian accent, "Good afternoon, lads. My name is Mr. Lloyds. Now, I'll get straight to the point. The thing is, an emergency has arisen. Attacks and raids are moving to the southern part of France. The three of you need to get out of the country as soon as possible. I want you boys to go down this trapdoor. After walking for about half a mile, you three will come to a big door. Knock on it firmly thrice. Then, someone will ask you lads for the password. It is 'maggots' [a shoddy one, I know]. Further instructions will be given after you three are granted access through the door."

If this incident would have taken place a few months before it did, I would have never agreed to follow the man's instructions. But, things were becoming so potty that I readily said yes to go down first. I went over to the trapdoor and peered inside. I could make out the outline of a staircase. The man shoved his beefy hand inside his pocket and produced a small torch. He handed it to me, gave us a quick wave and walked out of the cottage, whistling a tune.

I clicked the torch open and shone the beam inside the trapdoor. I could clearly see a short staircase and a narrow path leading away from it. "Should we wait for Mr. Lloyds?" I asked. Will shook his head. I inhaled deeply and went inside.

The stairs weren't big, so I had to walk very carefully. After I was halfway down the staircase, I heard a grunt and the crunching of gravel. I turned around and saw Martin climbing down. I flashed him the 'thumbs-up' sign, but I gestured too soon. Martin, like a prize idiot, stumbled and practically toppled down the stairs, sending me crashing down to the ground. I landed hard on my back. I heard an ugly crack as soon as my back made contact with the hard, ruthless ground. I had evidently broken something. And of course, the torch just *had* to get thrown away from my hand and break. We were left in complete darkness.

"Can't you climb down a flight of stairs properly, you absolute prat?!" I cried. He opened his mouth and brought out profuse apologies. I rolled my eyes at him and said, "I've broken something, you dolt. How am I supposed to get to our destination, whatever it is?" I could hear Will coming down. He spotted me lying on the ground and rushed to my side.

"Are you alright, pal?" He asked. I made a face. I could hear Will chuckling. "What the *hell* is so comical?" I asked angrily. You know how I hate being laughed at. "Martin landed you good and proper, did he?" He asked.

"You weren't so willing to laugh back up in that cottage, were you?" I asked. His laughter ceased. I smirked and tried to sit up. A searing pain ran through my back and I had to lie down again. "What do we do now?" Martin asked. I was about to let him know that as he was the one who had landed us in a situation, he should be the one to think fast and find a solution, when I felt a muscular hand under my knees and another on the portion of my back just below my shoulders. The next second, I was hoisted onto Will's shoulder. I gasped in shock.

"Will, what are you doing?"

"I'm carrying you, you blind bat."

"Let's call Mr. Lloyds."

"No use. He'll be far away by now."

"How do you reckon that one out?"

"There is a secret passage in the bathroom of that cottage."

"But still, I don't think you'll be able to carry me for long, Will."

Will smirked and began running as easily as if I were made of mere cotton. I was, needless to say, astounded. "H-How can you run so fast with me on your shoulder?"

"Never mind about that. If you thought, even for a second, that I was going to leave you grovelling in the dust over there, you don't know a single thing about me.

After some walking, we reached a massive mahogany door, just like Mr. Lloyds had said. It looked rather impeding. I could hear muffled chatter beyond the door. Martin raised his hand and knocked firmly on it thrice. We could hear swift footsteps coming towards the door. A second later, a voice from inside asked, "Password?" Will responded, "Maggots; if you ask me, it's a horrible choice." The door swung open.

A tall and highly muscular man stood before us [he looked like an Olympic wrestler]. He had bushy brown hair and a pencil moustache. His eyes were dark brown- almost black. He held up a spirit lamp in his weather-beaten hand. He raised his eyebrows slightly when he caught sight of Will carrying me. I glared at him [I was as embarrassed as sin]. He looked away from me and said in a firm tone, "Follow me." [Some instructions, huh?]

The man led us down a dark and craggy corridor. Martin asked him what his name was, and he replied in a stock tone, "Kenneth Brown." There was a horrible moment on the way when Will tripped over a few loose stones and almost lost his balance. If he would have fallen, I would have been gifted with a blood-spewing mini volcano on my head.

Finally, Brown hand-signed to us to halt. He squatted and, placing the lamp beside him, opened a trapdoor that was set into the ground. "Be careful with him," Brown said, tilting his head towards me. Will nodded and ordered, "Martin, help me." Martin grabbed my legs [the Duke of Leicester actually held my legs ;)] and the two of them began walking down the stairs leading from the trapdoor, carrying me carefully.

"Don't let me fall," I warned the duo [but, while saying it, I was looking only at Your Dukeness]. Will mocked, "Don't worry, *sweet patootie*, we'll put you in your crib the sunny side up." I rolled my eyes. Will went inside first, backwards. Then, Martin walked inside. A pungent odour met my nostrils the second we entered, and I scrunched my nose up.

"You look like my old Aunt Mildred, Lew," laughed Will.

"You obviously aren't too sensible when it comes to commenting about people on their looks," I retorted.

My voice came out horribly nasal. Will guffawed loudly, sounding like an obese whale or something. When I told him exactly what I thought of him, he called me a 'damn goody-two-shoes'. For the first half of the walk down, everything was fine. I was no doubt uncomfortable, but at least I did not break anything. And then, *it* happened.

As I was being carried down, out of bloody nowhere, a goddamn *adder* showed up and sodding *lashed out* at me. Now, ever since I was a cute, innocent child of no more than five years, I have been absolutely *paranoid* of snakes. They drive me mad!

So, when one struck out at me like that, I gave out a mortified yell. My bellow startled Martin, who dropped me suddenly [he certainly was a danger to my bones]. With a sickening crunch, my heels collided against a stair. I yelled once more.

Brown sighed in exasperation and said, "Carry him quickly. We'll reach in a few minutes." Martin picked my legs up again and he and Will quickened their pace. I was still in a state of panic, not to mention in horrible pain. Sparks did some kind of a Spanish dance in front of my eyes.

"Infernal reptiles," I cursed under my breath. I shut my eyes tightly and asked, in a voice barely more than a whisper, "Has it gone?" Martin laughed slightly and replied, "I think so." I breathed in and out, trying to get my racing pulse to slow down. "It was not a poisonous one," Brown declared, glaring down at me. I shrugged to the best of my abilities.

A few minutes later, I heard footsteps coming towards us. "Someone's coming," I announced. "We're not blind," snapped Will.

After some moments, a beam of light came into my view. It was followed by two men. They advanced towards us, the worried expressions on their faces clearly visible due to the illumination provided by the torch with them.

"What happened?" The older one among the two asked an anxious look in his blue eyes. "Nothing too bad, McCartney; one of the lads has gotten himself into some pain." Their gazes flickered over to me. "Come on, then, boy," McCartney said, grabbing my legs. The other male, who looked like he was in his late teens and was most probably McCartney's son, took my shoulders, and I was not-so-royally carried forward.

The youth smirked, "Mum'll have a cow when she looks at him." McCartney shook his head and said,

"He needs to be given proper treatment. The women will look after him well."

It must have been only a few minutes later that we reached our final destination, but to me it seemed like a whole hour. Time always treats us so unfairly- whenever we want it to pass quickly, it ticks by slowly and when we want it to slow down a bit, it gallops away.

I was hurt very badly. My heels as well as my back were throbbing with unbearable pain. Cursing the stupid adder, I tried to settle into a comfortable position.

Finally, to my mad joy [;)], we reached our destination, which turned out to be three rooms that looked like the home of a Jemma Dear. Everything was sinfully clean, the walls were painted a shade of pink that should, in my not-so-humble opinion, be made illegal and the curtains had pictures of plump cats with ribbons tied tightly around their necks. The person who had designed them was clearly not an Animal Rights supporter. In short, it was quite similar to the cottage with the Kathy Hep poster. However, I felt that the cottage was a lot better than this underground shelter because it had posters of *actresses*, and not cats, on the walls. I mean, who wants to stare at felines all day? So much so for the British Military. Also, as it was underground, our shelter was extremely stuffy.

As soon as we barged in like heroes on a film set, a woman ran into the room from another door [looking rather like the distraught heroine of our motion picture] and put a hand to her mouth as soon as she saw me. "My sweet Lord!" She cried, her green eyes flashing with shock. "He needs medical attention immediately!" [*Shocker*!]

The woman was followed by a girl who looked like she was about my age. She was an inch or two shorter than the woman, who could only be her mother. The girl had her mother's green eyes, but her chocolate-brown curls were like her father's. Somehow, I found myself remarking under my breath that her eyes complemented her hair much better than her mother's eyes did her own blond locks.

However, before I could give another thought as to why I did that, I was dragged inside a room and put on a bed smaller than the indoor snooker table at Candling Manor.

I groaned silently to myself. I knew I was going to be fussed over- another thing I loathe. The woman, who quickly introduced herself as Mrs. Evangeline McCartney, started bandaging my heels. The youth, who told us that he was named James McCartney, handed me a few pain killers. They made me want to vomit my intestines out- the sight of Martin surrounded by those repulsive empty bottles was still fresh in my mind.

Finally, after a good [BAD] half an hour, I was left to my own devices. I whistled 'April in Paris' as my eyes scanned the entire room. There was a small cupboard in one corner and a writing desk in another. It was congested but at least we were safe in here.

Suddenly, the door opened and the girl stepped in, holding a flask of water. At that moment, I hadn't the slightest clue why; I started feeling conscious of my appearance. I realized how untidy and sweaty I was. I tried to press the feeling down, but it kept resurfacing stubbornly.

She smiled at me and I grinned back at her. I couldn't help but notice the dimples that formed on her cheeks when a smile adorned her countenance. She placed the flask on the tiny table beside my bed.

"Hello, my name is Lewis," I introduced myself. "What's yours?" She replied, "I am January McCartney." Before I could stop myself, I found myself saying, "That's a nice name." "Thank you," she said, smiling again. "Listen, if you need anything, do not hesitate to call out, fine?" "Don't worry. I'll be tip-top," I answered.

"Hey, by the way, your luggage has arrived. Would you like me to haul it inside for you?"

I shook my head and replied, "No, my bags are heavy. You'll dislocate your shoulders."

After I said that, I almost wished I hadn't, because January turned on her heel [hers was not smashed into smithereens] and left the room wordlessly. I felt like kicking myself [I would have, too, if my heels didn't hurt like nobody's business]. I had most probably offended her. However, after a minute or two, the knob turned and the door swung open.

My eyebrows shot up in surprise. Standing in the doorway was January, my suitcases in her hand. She shot me a look and entered the room, carrying luggage I had struggled with without any effort.

She placed it beside my bed and straightened up, her green eyes boring into my brown ones. "Never underestimate anyone," she told me, the corners of her mouth going slightly upwards. "You never know what the person in front of you is capable of accomplishing."

"Yes, ma'am," I said, giving a two-fingered salute. I expected her to say something else, but I was proved wrong. She simply smiled that dimply smile of hers for what seemed to the younger and much more vulnerable me like the umpteenth time and left the room, her curls swishing behind her.

Chapter 21
A El Diablo

The next two days [I know that we were underground, but Brown told us that he would keep on predicting how much time had passed with the help of his watch and keep on informing us about it, I lost track of time the second we reached our shelter] saw me getting better and better under the care of the sweet January McCartney.

The McCartney family was under threat from Hitler too [obviously] because Mr. McCartney had caused an uproar in the German offices by blowing up quite a bit of Research Department Explosive.

Returning to January, I told her all about myself. I didn't know why, but I felt like I could safely trust her. Will, Martin, James and I spoke together for long hours about the war that would most probably follow how 'twittish' the Germans were, how Britain would kick their rears badly if a war ensued and our favourite flavours of candy.

Our food rations were meagre- our meals usually consisted of a loaf of bread and half a teaspoon of hardened butter. Also, Will's birthday came on the second day of us being in the shelter. None of us knew when his birthday was, so we got a shock when he just walked up to breakfast and said, "It's my birthday today. So sue me."

I went up to him and gave him a few pennies as his gift [I made a mental note to give him something after we got out of the 'Hitler Mess', as we named it] and asked, "So, you are seventeen years old now, right?" He took the money from my hand and stated plainly, "Nineteen years young."

My eyes almost jumped out of their respective sockets. I realised that I had never asked Will how old he was before. When I asked Martin his age, he replied, "Eighteen." To be honest with you, I wasn't delighted to know that I was the youngest among the three of us.

One of the many downsides of living in such a small place was that I had to share a bed with Will and Martin and, let me tell you, it was *not* a pleasant experience. Martin didn't cease kicking me and Will practically ensured that I stayed awake the whole night with his sleep-talking. He kept saying something that sounded like 'nuts and berries, waggy waggy'.

So, I was compelled to sleep on a mattress laid on the floor. However, I was no longer getting nightmares, which was a good sign. Honestly, those things had taken away my sleep on many occasions [I do NOT mean Christmas and Thanksgiving].

On the fourth day, Brown called us all together and said, "We have to leave this place in two days at the most. We cannot stay underground forever. We have to reach Switzerland at all costs. Therefore, I have prepared a plan of action. We shall leave the day after tomorrow for Italy. We cannot cross the France-Switzerland border as it is too dangerous to go there at the moment. In Italy, we shall travel through the Alps and, traversing under St. Gotthard Pass, we shall enter Switzerland. There, we shall split."

"Waitaminnit! You don't expect us to walk all the way up to Switzerland, do you?" Will asked, scandalised.

Brown looked at Will and said coolly, "Yes, I do. As all of you must have figured out by now, we shall be walking through underground passages. These passages have been specially made by experienced army officers. We will need stamina, strength and determination, but it can be done. I did it when I was younger than you."

"But our legs will go for a full toss! We'll die of cramps!"

"No such things will happen if you walk properly. I agree that it is a tedious task, but it is the safest thing we can do at this point in time."

Will opened his mouth to protest, but Brown cut him off, "Please try to understand. As I said before, it is the only thing we can do now. Anyway, allow me to continue. The McCartney family will go to Zurich and the three boys will take shelter in Geneva. In your respective shelters, you all shall be protected from danger and harm. However, on the way, we will have to carry our luggage with us." We all nodded and looked at each other. The plan sounded foolproof, but was it one of the 'easier-said-than-done' cases?

James asked, "And what about you, Brown?" Brown squared his shoulders and, a manic light coming into his brown eyes, he replied gruffly, "If at all there is a war-it seems very probable-I shall fight and teach those Nazi scoundrels a thing or two. If there is no war, I will continue working with my comrades to create a new, safe and peaceful world for all of us."

I have to admit, I was rather impressed by him. In fact, believe it or not, I almost felt *ashamed* about the fact that I was not going to fight. I quickly pressed down that feeling, reminding myself about the dream I had cherished for so many years.

My wounds kept getting better and better, and so did my friendship with January McCartney. After knowing her only for a few days, I could safely add her to my list of close friends. She was very unlike some other girls I had met in the past. Some of Candling's friends have daughters and they brought them over to our house when they visited us. And I have to admit, I had never been impressed with any of them. They all acted like spoilt cranky brats.

But, January was different. She was trustworthy and very easy to get along with. With her merry eyes, optimistic attitude and kind heart, she made for a very good person indeed. Also, I found out from her brother that she was very talented- she was apparently a very good writer and artist. I still felt that weird feeling whenever she was around, though. For example, she walked in to change my bandages on the second day and I told her she looked nice with her hair let down. Her cheeks turned bright red and I was feeling rather strange. She hurriedly replaced my bandages, mumbled something under her breath and all but sprinted out of the room. A moment after she left hastily, Will and Martin entered the room, maddeningly superior smirks on their faces.

When I asked them what the matter was, they simply grinned widely. Honestly, I felt like thrashing the Nick out of the pair of them. "What the Dickens is the matter with you two?" I asked impatience evident in my tone. Martin sat down on my bed and answered, "Oh...nothing's wrong with *us*. It's just that you've caught something." "Do you really need to add to my grievances at the moment?" I asked wearily.

Will placed his hands on my shoulders and said, "But this...*thing* that you've managed to catch is not very grieving. In fact, it's one of life's pleasures. So, enjoy it." And before I could say a word more on the topic, Will began talking about whether tomatoes were fruits or vegetables.

Perhaps sooner than I expected, the day of our departure dawned [though we couldn't see the sun; we were underground]. I woke very early in the day, a jittery feeling coursing through my veins. I tried to fall asleep again, but nervousness acted as a barrier between me and slumber. I had been through a lot of problems. I had taken risks. I didn't want to take any more and I certainly wanted to keep trouble away. I was tired of everything. I just wanted to get out of the whirlpool of danger I was stuck in and lead a normal life.

My mind travelled back to when I was thirteen years of age. Back then, I would have loved to get stuck in such a situation. Of course, that was due to the countless adventure books I used to read. At that time, I would have given absolutely everything to be caught up in an adventure such as the one I was stuck in. Oh, how innocently idiotic I was!

Breakfast that day was a rather solemn affair. I was carried to the table by Brown and made to sit on a chair. "He should be brought out of his cocoon of rest," he had said. My back hurt like sin, and I kept on wishing to go back to the bed in the miniscule room I slept in.

At the table, no one spoke much. Will cracked a few jokes to light up the atmosphere, but no one laughed. Everyone was far too tensed about what lay ahead of us. Martin didn't touch a morsel. When Brown wheedled him to have at least a few pieces of bacon, he protested snappishly. Judging by the green tinge on his cheeks, he had been sick early in the morning. I felt sorry for him.

James was absently sucking on his fork and staring at the ceiling, his eyes glazed. Mr. and Mrs. McCartney were eating silently, without lifting their gazes from their plates. January was doing the same. As for me, I was nervous beyond all compare. I tried taking deep breaths and counting in my head, but the butterflies in my stomach didn't stop fluttering about. In fact, I was hardly sure if they could even qualify as butterflies any more. They felt more like albatrosses. There we were; all eight of us, headed towards El Diablo, extremely unsure whether we would live to tell our story or not.

Chapter 22

SWEET DREAMS

We moved out of our little underground shelter at precisely twenty one minutes past eight. I was laid on a hand-made stretcher. The other men took turns to carry me. January and Brown carried spirit lamps for the [obvious] purpose of illumination.

We passed through plenty of rocky little underground passages. At some places, the ceiling stooped so low that the others had to bend down until their noses were a few inches away from their knees and move. The ones who carried my stretcher during the 'low-ceiling' times had to literally duck-walk.

The lack of sunlight and stuffy atmosphere was taking its toll on all of us. I felt hot and horribly sticky. My head started aching slightly. The pain in my heels and back and Will's grumbling was not helping matters out. But, most of all I was ashamed that my friends had to carry me. I was slowing everyone down. My discomfort was too much to handle. I closed my eyes and tried to drop off. However, sleep seemed reluctant to come to me. Finally, after what seemed like hours to me, I fell asleep.

He stood on the platform with a painfully erect posture and surveyed his soldiers, his hands clasped together behind his back and his feet wide apart. There was a fire blazing in his beady eyes- the fire of the desire to achieve victory. Scores and scores of Nazi soldiers stood before him, rifles in their hands and determined looks on their faces. One glance at them was sufficient to tell me that they meant business.

"Go, my Nazis! Go and fight courageously for all that you are worth! Fight until the last breath in your body leaves you!" Adolf Hitler yelled, punching the air in front of him, his fist clenched. "Do this, my faithful warriors, and we can conquer the world! Those English rats are nothing in front of us. Do your best, men, and victory will surely be ours!" Applause erupted from his audience. With perfect co-ordination, the soldiers raised their rifles and bellowed, "For the Nazis!"

That scene dissolved into another one...

I was standing on a battlefield. A fierce war was raging all around me. Soldiers were shooting and stabbing each other. Corpses fell down onto the ground with dull thuds. Blood spurted in all directions as if it were mere water. War-cries echoed all around the air.

There was bloodlust and wild frenzy everywhere. It was horrible. And in the middle of all the violence, tough and erect, coolly sweeping his gaze over the bedlam was Lord Ares. He was in full war regalia. His dark curls leaked out of his helmet and framed his handsome face. The massive hounds at his feet threw back their heads and began howling. And, at that very moment, Lord Ares turned his head and looked straight at me. My legs turned to lead as his ruby-coloured eyes bore deep into my being. He opened his mouth and spoke, in a deep voice that rang with authority, "You must fulfil your destiny."

"Lewis, wake up!" I heard Martin's voice asking me to emerge out of the realms of slumber. Two strong arms began shaking me. I blinked my eyes open. After a few woozy seconds, I realised that I was on the ground and not being carried. "And a very good morning to you, too," grinned Will. I gave a lop-sided smile. "Morning, you two! How are we doing?" "According to Brown, rather well," replied Will. "For how long have I been asleep?" I asked [don't look like that! My curiosity is a trait I have inherited from my Grandpa Hargreaves!].

"Oh, for about an hour," replied Will airily. "We stopped here for a respite. But, Brown has said that we will be going above-ground in a short while. Of course, we can't stay down here for long without any fresh air, we'll all get our R.I.Ps served to us." said Martin. I heard James call from some distance away, "Has lazy bones woken up yet?" Martin replied in the affirmative and turned to me. "Brown wants you sitting up," he said. I groaned, "But I've broken my back, for Shakespeare's sake! I'm officially an invalid!"

Without a word, Will grasped me and, in one fluid movement, shifted me into an upright position. It was unbearably painful. I had to bite my tongue to stop the yell that was about to emanate from my mouth. My back was aching like there was no tomorrow. I looked at Brown, who was standing a few yards away and talking to Mr. McCartney, and cursed him mentally.

After I was done calling him all the swear-words I knew, I turned away from him. Mrs. McCartney and January were sitting down close to where Brown, James and Mr. McCartney were conversing.

I looked at Martin, who cleared his throat and said, "Hey, Lewis. Just before Will and I woke you up, you were muttering something in your sleep. You were going on and on about destiny!" "Martin is right, chum. Are you planning on becoming a fortune-teller or something?" Will asked.

He stood up and, moving his hands in a haphazard fashion, said in the raspy tone the crystal-ball-readers and fortune-tellers always use, "Your fate says that you will become someone great in your life, but your destiny indicates towards your becoming a court jester! My, my, my, this is confusing indeed! I'm sure you don't count dressing up in a white and black one-piece and turning cartwheels and telling poor jokes to entertain the court as greatness.

Cross my palm with silver and I shall reveal more, much more!"

Martin burst into laughter. I allowed myself a few expressions of mirth as well. James came over to us and slapped Will on his back. "Are you considering a new career, Fergusson?" He grinned. 'Nah, McCartney! I'm jus', y'know, goofing around!" The two of them banged knuckles and James sat down, grinning.

Martin looked at me and asked, "Lewis, can you tell us why you were muttering 'destiny' in your sleep?" I shrugged and looked down. I didn't really want to tell them about my bad dreams. Will punched my shoulder and said, "C'mon, mate, prattle it out, will ya?" I opened my mouth to say something, when James said, "If you just tell us all about the whole deal, you'll feel a whole lot better. Trust me, pal, I speak from experience."

"I really don't think I want to share my dreams."

Martin said, "Let's take a quick vote. Who's for Lewis speaking up?" Will, James and Martin raised their hands. The first two smirked. I rolled my eyes and decided to give in.

"Fine, I'll tell you boys. I've been having these, y'know, *nightmares*," I said. The other lads looked at each other and then at me. "Do you remember any of them? Something?" James asked. "Yes, I do," I replied. "I remember all of them fully."

"That is strange," Martin said, rubbing his chin. "People generally tend to forget most of their dreams after being awake for two minutes."

"Whatever, shut up, Martin! Lewis must be special or summat. Let him continue!" Will snapped.

And, I related the two nightmares I had that night to them, my mind hoping to hell that they would have some interpretations for them.

Chapter 23

Off Again

After I finished telling my friends about the two dreams I had, I looked at all of them expectantly. Will and James had clueless expressions on their faces. Martin, however, was gazing at me thoughtfully.

"These dreams must surely mean something," he said.

"Oh come on, Tins!" Will said. "Are you trying to say that Lew here is having some kind of nocturnal telepathic visions?" "Well, that could very well be the case!" Martin argued. "For all that we know, Lewis's nightmares may be messages!"

"Yo, the nightly postal service has done a great job," Will retorted, sarcasm dripping in big dollops off his words. He turned to James and the two of them began a separate conversation about radio programmes.

Martin rolled his eyes and turned to look at me. He said, "Lewis, like I said before, I think your dreams are conveying something to you. You really should have told me about them earlier." I simply shrugged.

Martin took a deep breath before continuing, "Lewis, I have good reason to believe that a fully-fledged war is not far off. You saw Lord Ares on that battlefield, right? His presence definitely symbolises chaotic violence and carnage. Moreover, the war was between England and Germany. What else can it all mean? As for the 'fulfil your destiny' part, well, I do not know what it means."

"That's the thing that puzzles me the most," I said. "Have you had any other besides the two you just told us about?" I nodded my head and proceeded to tell him about the rest of the bad dreams that constantly invaded my sleep. When I came to the one in which Will was shooting that woman, I lowered my voice. I didn't want the Fergusson lad to know that I had been having such a dream about him.

"Hmmm...Well..." Martin said, his chin resting on his hand and his blue eyes staring off into space. "I really don't know what to make of these. Maybe we'll find out later. But, if you get any more such dreams, please notify me immediately."

"Yessir, Captain!" I said, mock-saluting him. He shook his head in the 'oh-you'll-never-improve' style. At that very moment, I saw January coming towards us, two plastic mugs in her hands. I grinned at her and waved, realising only a second later how absolutely idiotic I must have looked. She smiled back at me as she placed the two mugs down before us.

They were filled to the brim with tea. "I made it with tea-bags and the hot water from Father's thermos flask," she smiled. "I'll get the other two mugs in a moment."With that, she turned and walked off.

I grinned at her retreating form and looked to the right, only to see that the mugs were empty. Will smirked at me, his hazel eyes holding a teasing expression. His lips were laced with the beverage the mugs had held not a minute ago. "What?" I asked, slightly annoyed by the look in his eyes.

"Nothing, idiot," he replied, his smirk widening. James looked at Will and an annoyingly superior expression appeared on his visage. The truth dawned upon me after ten whole seconds [I know, I'm rather slow]. The two of them had gulped the tea down first, making Martin and I wait until January came again. I shook my fist at the two block-heads. They simply roared with laughter.

At that moment, January returned with two more mugs. She kept them down carefully, picked both the empty ones up and walked off.

I grabbed a mug before Will could get anywhere near it and began drinking from it like a drunkard downs his fifth bottle of single malt whiskey. Out of the corner of my eye, I saw Martin slapping James's hand away from the remaining container of tea.

"You've already had one," Martin said, his tone taking on a fierce edge. "All right, all right," James said, patting Martin's shoulder as he did so. "Don't flip your wig." "I don't wear a wig, you ass. I, very much unlike you, have naturally handsome hair," huffed Martin. He got up and marched off to where the elders and January were sitting. James stared after him, looking rather blank. "Since when did hair start becoming *handsome*?" He asked.

"I really don't know about that, James, but Martin evidently does," I replied.

"And why did he storm off in such an evil mood?"

"He loves his mop."

"Oh, I see."

James eyed the remaining mug of tea and said, a little slyly, "Well, since he doesn't seem to desire it..." He grabbed the mug and gulped the tea down in one. Will grinned at him and said, "Y'know, you're incorrigible." "Nah," said James, licking his lips. "I'm simply McCartney!" Will laughed and the two of them banged knuckles [again].

At that moment, Brown walked over to us. He said in his firm voice, "We're continuing on our way in five minutes. Please make sure that you all have wrapped everything up and are ready by then. I don't want anything important being left back here. And, just so you boys know, we'll be reaching a ground-port soon. (Brown seemed to know everything like magic!)"

"Fabulous!" Will exclaimed, clapping his hands together.

[Reader, let me explain to you what exactly a groundport is. The term may be new to you. To put it to you in a few words, it is an opening in an underground passage through which you can go above the ground. Good, right?]

Brown cleared his throat and spoke, "By the way, have the three of you said something derogatory to that Martin lad? He is in rather a bad mood."

"Oh, don't worry about him, Brown. He's just very slightly nuts. He'll be alreet and dancing with bobby soxers before you can say 'cor'," said Will, gesticulating comically with his hands. Brown rolled his eyes and walked away, muttering something under his breath about 'how the English language was shooting down the slope of the younger generation of the British civilisation'. Will guffawed, clutching his sides in mirth. James grinned and said, "Let's start 'wrapping everything up', as Brown himself put it."

In five minutes, we were ready to leave. James went ahead to lead the way with his father and Brown. I was unceremoniously dumped onto the stretcher by Will. "Hey man, I hope you know that you can be gentler with me," I told him indignantly. He raised his eyebrows at me and said, "The last time I checked, you were a teenager made of bones and sinew and not a fragile doll comprised of china." I opened my mouth to protest, but closed it again, deciding that arguing with Will was pointless.

After a minute, Martin came walking briskly to us. "I have been kindly instructed by Mr. Brown to aid you, Master Fergusson, in carrying this stretcher," he said haughtily.

From my horizontal position on the stretcher, I couldn't very well give him a classic puzzled look, but I tried to accomplish that feat nevertheless. Will was trying hard to control his laughter. "Pray excuse me, but how are you, Master Candling?" Martin asked me.

Suddenly, it hit me that I had never told Martin that I was [and still am] a Lord. I figured that no one else had told him either because he didn't address me as 'Lord', which I am sure he would have done.

"Er...yes, Martin, I'm top," I said. Martin cleared his throat. "That is, if you exclude my heels and my back," I added grudgingly. "That is certainly more truthful, Master Candling," said Martin. I rolled my eyes.

At that very second, Will lost all the control that he had over his emotions. With an explosive snort that sounded more like a Mount Vesuvius eruption, he began roaring with laughter. Tears of mirth leaked out of his hazel eyes. I sighed in an exasperated fashion and asked, "Are you two buffoons going to carry this damn stretcher or not? Will, when in the name of tarnation, are you going to stop laughing your head off?"

Will, gasping for breath, replied, "Well, I can see only one of the two buffoons you just mentioned, Lewis; where is the other?" I rolled my eyes again and said, "I'm in no mood for your silly jokes, Will. Now, *are the two of you going to pick this bloody thing up*?"

Chapter 24

Above Ground

"A long time ago, some year in the seventeenth century, there was a woman named Victoria Thorn. When she was twenty years old, she lived all alone in a small wooden cottage that was in the middle of a dense forest. She had flowing hair that was jet-black and striking green eyes. Her skin was as pale as a ghost. And of course, there was one more thing about her: She hated humans.

"Now, though she detested humans, Victoria absolutely loved animals. She could talk to all of them, she could. Also, she was very good with herbs and could concoct potions with amazing skill. One day, a young man named Sebastian Archer accidentally came across her humble abode. Filled with curiosity, he peeped inside her cottage through one of the windows.

"Victoria was standing inside with her back to Archer. A bubbling cauldron stood slightly to her left. Victoria was chanting some incantations and adding a variety of herbs and powders to the cauldron. Archer came to the conclusion that Victoria was a witch.

"In those days, witch-hunting was very popular. Innocent girls as young as four were suspected to be witches and burned at the stake. Archer, acting impulsively and irrationally, took his hunting knife out of its holder, took aim and threw it at the oblivious Victoria.

"Victoria gave out a piercing shriek and fell to the floor, the long knife in her back. Archer ran inside her cottage to raid it. As he was stuffing everything that was valuable in his eyes into his sack, he saw out of the corner of his eye that Victoria was moving slightly.

"He went over to her. Blood was pouring out of the wound in her back. There was very little life left in her. Archer pulled his bloody knife out of her back and stabbed her again and again, while Victoria gasped for mercy. Then, he grabbed his sack and ran away, the knife with which he had murdered Victoria Thorn back in its holder.

"Archer reached home late that night. He kept his sack and knife in his back room and retired for the night. The next morning, Archer woke up early. He went downstairs, had his breakfast and entered his back room, expecting to find his things there. However, there was no trace of his sack or of his guilty knife. Archer searched high and low for them, but he could not locate them. They had simply vanished into thin air.

"Highly puzzled and even more annoyed, Archer entered his privy to have a bath, hoping that the stimulating feel of hot water would soothe his nerves. However, the moment he entered the privy, he froze. Standing in front of him, with a mysterious smile on her face, was none other than Victoria Thorn. A few hours later, Archer was found dead in his privy, cuts, bruises and scratches all over his body."

I raised my eyebrows at Will as he finished telling us his 'horror' story. "Wow," I said. "That was *boring*." "Hey, come on!" Will said, looking offended. I shrugged, but the action hurt my back, so I stopped doing it in a millisecond.

"It was rather modest," said Martin, his nose high in the air. Will, whatever I said about his story slipping from his mind like water off a duck's back, guffawed loudly. Turning slightly, I saw that Brown was serving the hazel-eyed boy his 'you-better-dig-your-grave' glare. Will put his hand over his mouth and chortled away to glory. I heard Martin mutter under his breath something that sounded like 'I, for the life of me, do not know what to do with that young man'. I grinned. He had clearly not emerged out of his 'Duke' mood.

After travelling for another five minutes, Brown walked over to us, his lamp in his left hand. "We shall be stopping in a minute," he said briskly, getting straight to the point. "What? Again?" asked Will, looking scandalised. Brown gave him his capital glare again and replied sternly, "Yes, Fergusson, *again*; unless you do not want to live to see your twentieth birthday."

Realisation dawned upon Will's countenance. He exclaimed, "Oh...we're going to be going above-ground!" "Yes, Fergusson, we are," Brown said and walked away, taking big strides.

"Brilliant!" Will exclaimed, ecstatic. "I'm so happy I could do a Spanish two-step here and now!"I rolled my eyes and asked him, imitating Brown's voice, "Can you even dance, Fergusson?" "Of course I can!" He replied and began doing something that was so odd that no combination of the twenty-six alphabets of the English language can accurately describe it.

"I must kindly ask you to cease behaving in such a manner, Master Fergusson." "And I must kindly ask *you* to shut your hole and sod off," said Will, irritated. "Really, Martin, it was funny at first, but now it's very annoying. Just drop this high-and-mighty manner of yours, alreet? You're just a simple British lad, not the son of a Duke or summat!"

I had to use up all of my self-control to refrain from letting Will know that Martin was indeed the son of a Duke. Martin simply avoided Will's gaze and appeared to be very interested in the ground. A rather awkward silence followed this, and I had two reasons to be glad when we finally went above the ground.

Will jumped three feet into the air and twirled like an experienced ballerina. "Aah...I love air! I love air! I love air!" He sang, flapping his arms around like an albatross. Brown rolled his eyes at him. I was sitting in a corner, propped up against an oak tree. My back hurt, but the pain was more bearable now.

The McCartneys were sitting directly across from me and talking amongst themselves. James had a sulky expression on his face. I could make out that he wanted to fool around with Will instead of chatting with his parents and sister. Brown was pacing around, a grim expression on his visage. Martin was sitting a few yards away from the McCartney family, his blue eyes staring off into space.

I smiled to myself; making the most of the 21 percent of oxygen around me [God only knows how I have managed to keep the composition of air in my mind]. Suddenly, something in the grass beside me caught my eye. I reached out for it with my left hand and closed my fingers around it. When I withdrew my appendage, I saw that it was a badge with the Nazi Swastika on it!

All of a sudden, the grass behind me rustled. It was highly queer as there was no breeze blowing at that time. I turned around as quickly as I could, just in time to see the heel of a brown boot disappear behind a tight group of trees. A horrible thought entered my mind. What if the Nazi badge and the person hiding were connected [I know, I know. I'm a bit too slow]?

I could not decide what to do. I didn't want to shout out, because that action of mine would surely make whoever it was behind the trees flee. But, how else could I attract the attention of the others?

Thankfully, Brown came to my rescue. His sharp military senses had made him aware of the presence behind the trees. With absolutely fantabulous skill, he climbed onto one of the boughs of the tree against which I was propped. He motioned to the others in our group and me to maintain silence. The person hiding behind the trees was at the same disadvantage as us- we couldn't see him, but *he* couldn't see *us* either.

The others came close to the tree I was taking support of as quietly as they could. I watched, my heart in my mouth, as Brown extended his right leg and wrapped it around another branch. A second later, he was hanging from the second limb. Then, with the help of his left arm, he grabbed another branch and swung over to it. I was absolutely amazed with his dexterity. Then, he did something that almost made me yell out loud. In one supple jump, he landed straight behind the cluster of trees!

There was a loud yell. A moment later, Brown emerged from the other side of the trees, pulling a soldier by his collar. The latter was wearing a Nazi uniform that was torn in some places. He wore a helmet. I could clearly figure that he had no weapons with him except for a small and blunt-looking pocket-knife. Through the vision-slit in the soldier's head-gear, I could see that his eyes were hazel.

January gasped, clasping her hand over her mouth. She looked [and she most probably was] scared stiff. Martin looked frightened too.

Mr. McCartney went over to the soldier and gripped his right shoulder, ensuring his highly low chances of escape. Brown, his face holding a furious expression, pulled off the soldier's helmet. When I saw his face, I was astounded out of my wits. The soldier looked exactly [and I mean exactly] like Will!

I turned to look at the said youth. He looked flabbergasted out of his wits and his mouth was wide open with shock.

"Who are you?" Brown asked, beside himself with rage. The soldier remained silent. "WHO ARE YOU?" Brown yelled, shaking his shoulder roughly. The soldier gulped and answered, "Spencer Fergusson."

Chapter 25
My Only Family

The next few minutes passed by in a whirlwind. Brown and Mr. McCartney pulled Spencer underground. I was carried haphazardly by James and Martin. January and her mother followed us down. Will brought up the rear. I couldn't see him from my position, but I could very well imagine the stunned expression on his face.

After moving for around two minutes, we halted. Brown and Mr. McCartney dumped Spencer Fergusson onto the rough ground. James and Martin sat me down in such a way that my back was leaning against the wall of the passage that was opposite to the wall at which's foot Spencer Fergusson was sprawled.

"Why were you spying on us?" Brown asked, fury etched into his every syllable. Spencer remained silent. Brown repeated his question, clutching Spencer's collar.

"I...I was asked to by my seniors," replied the soldier. Brown kicked him hard and stood; his weathered face displayed nothing other than anger, as Spencer yelled his guts out. "Give us details," Mr. McCartney said crisply. Spencer gulped and choked out, "By my Nazi seniors."

Brown nothing short of roared. "Do not you have even an ounce of shame in you, you little piece of trash?" He yelled. "You, an Englishman, betrayed your country and are relating it like an infant confesses to stealing candies!" He raised his hand and hit Spencer straight across his face. January barely managed to stifle the scream that was on the verge of escaping from her lips. Mr. McCartney turned to his daughter and said, sternness ringing in his tone,

"This is how traitors are, and should be, treated. Once you betray your nation, you should expect no mercy, and certainly not any sympathy."

Suddenly, it struck me. The true sense of the whole thing revealed itself. The youth I had seen in my dream was not Will, but Spencer! The crying woman dressed in the red and cerulean robe was Mother England, and, by betraying her, Spencer was as good as shooting her.

Will stepped forth and said his lividness showing in his tone, "Explain all this to me right now, *Fergusson*." He spat the last word out in disgust. Spencer took a shuddering breath in and said, "You were told by everyone that your mother died while giving birth to you, Will. But..." However, before Spencer could complete his sentence, Will asked, pure venom dripping off his words, "How dare you address me by my name?" Spencer looked down at the ground. I saw tear tracks glistening on his cheeks.

Will extended his left leg and pushed Spencer's chin up with his toes. Spencer said, through gritted teeth, "She did not die while giving birth to you. That was a story made up to tell you. The truth is; she is still alive!"

"What?!" Will bellowed, pulling himself up to his full height. "How can you even think of lying at a time like this?" "But I am telling the truth," said Spencer. "Evelyn Fergusson is very much alive. She's in a bad condition, yes, but she's still living. As for me, I am your twin brother!"

Will kicked Spencer hard in his guts and questioned, "What in the name of bloody hell are you going on about, you arse?" "Listen to me," Spencer said, pleading edge coming to his voice. "When we were born in 1920, our family was in danger from German military men. So, Father suggested that we separate. You were going to stay at Cornwall Naval Defence Camp with Father and Daniel and I was to go halfway across the country with Mother and Uncle Steven. You three stayed safe and well. However, trouble encountered the three of us.

"We were confronted by German soldiers. Somehow, Mother and I managed to get away with only a few injuries. Uncle, however, was grievously hurt. He succumbed to his wounds a day later. Mother and I took shelter in the cottage of an old hermit. She thought that we were safely out of danger, but she was arrantly wrong. Germans found us only a few days later. They took us prisoner.

There, Mother was held hostage and I was forced to join the German army. They told me that if I didn't fight, then they would kill Mother. I...couldn't help it. I couldn't risk the life of my mother. She means the world to me. She-She's my only family."

I couldn't believe my ears. Lying on the ground before me was an injured boy, who had been forced to fight on the side of the Germans, by holding hostage the person he loved the most in the world. At that moment, I hated the Germans like I had never hated anyone or anything before.

Spencer continued, "I know that I have betrayed England. I know that I am a traitor. Above all, I know that I deserve to die for what I have done. Our nation comes before our family. I shouldn't have agreed to fight for the Germans. I am a sinner and I do not deny that fact." He shut his hazel eyes and began to pray. Silence hung around us. After a minute or two, he looked straight at Brown, and, meeting his gaze unflinchingly, said, "Shoot me."

Chapter 26

A Italia

I closed my eyes and braced myself, expecting to hear the sound of the gunshot that would be the end of Spencer. However, no such sound reached my ears. So, I slowly opened my eyes. Everyone was in the same position that they were in before I closed my eyes. For a few seconds, there was not a single sound to be heard.

Suddenly, Will dropped down to his knees and threw his arms around Spencer. "I'm sorry!" Will apologised in a trembling voice. "I am so sorry! Please forgive me!"

Spencer patted Will's back and consoled, "It's not your fault. If anyone should be saying sorry here, it is me."

Will was about to say something else, when Brown interrupted, "The story you have just shared with us is no doubt touching, young man, but I hope you comprehend that it does not help your position."

Will looked up, a pleading expression on his angular face. His lower lip was trembling badly. I could tell that he was making an effort to stop the tears that were threatening to escape his hazel eyes. "But he did it all for Mother!" he exclaimed, his voice cracking.

"Our nation comes before our family. I know that he did what he did to save the person he loves the most in this world, but a traitor is a traitor- no matter what." With that, he dug his hand into his pocket and fished out a six-shot revolver.

Will gasped, "No! You can't...You won't!" Spencer spoke, "Let him do it, Will. I deserve it." "No, you don't!" Will said fiercely. He turned to Brown and said, "How can you even *think* of doing away with him? He did it all because he loves his mother. Do you have the foggiest idea about how much a mother is worth?"

"So, isn't what Spencer did justified now?" Will yelled.

"No, it is not. Now please move, Fergusson. You are in my way," Brown said, cocking his revolver.

"I won't move even a millimetre," Will said, sticking his chin up in the air stubbornly.

"Now, Fergusson, try not to act like a petulant infant."

"Will, move," Spencer said weakly. "I told you- I completely deserve what I am going to get. You cannot obstruct the wheels of justice, Will. You cannot defend a criminal."

"I am not defending a criminal, because you aren't a criminal in the first place. And as for you, Brown, I am not moving my arse anywhere. If you want to shoot him, you will have to do it over my corpse."

Brown looked at Mr. McCartney, who looked at James. The next second, my McCartney friend and his father grabbed Will and pulled him, kicking and screaming, out of the way. The next second, before anyone could do anything, Brown pulled the trigger and the loud sound of a bullet making its escape from the barrel of a revolver met my ears, followed by a shout of, "I love you, Mother! Long live England!'.

The next few weeks passed by quickly. We walked through underground passages and caverns and went above-ground for air from time to time. On one of these 'air-breaks' [as we termed them], Brown got some medicines for my injuries from a British Military Forces Medical Outlet. And reader, their effects were nothing short of miraculous [They were much better than Dr. Hammond's Pills for Cold,

Temperature, Headache, Congestion and Sore Throat]. My back was getting better and better and my heels had almost recovered. With support, I could walk for quite some distances. However, memories of Spencer's death [murder, as Will put it] kept coming to my mind.

I have to admit, I wasn't very pleased with Brown. I believed Spencer had a good reason to do what he did, but Brown clearly did not second my thoughts.

I found myself thinking a lot about what Brown had done. Had he done the right thing by killing Spencer? Of course, Spencer was a traitor, but he had a good reason to do what he did. Was what Brown said really true? Was a traitor a traitor- no matter what? I have to admit, I didn't really expect Brown to just shoot Spencer like that.

Will was, as my great-aunt, Lucy Candling, would have put it, 'in a downright low mood'. He sulked about for the whole time and didn't say a word to anyone. Whenever anyone tried to talk to him, he answered with rudeness that would have made an old lady faint. However, I couldn't blame him- he had lost his twin brother, after all. Brown had suggested that we give Spencer a proper burial. So, Mr. McCartney, Brown and James had taken turns to dig a grave where Spencer was put to rest wrapped in a coat provided by Brown. Will watched from a distance, grief written all over his face.

As we proceeded on our way, temperatures dropped considerably. It was only logical, however, as we had begun traversing under the Alps. The walls of the passages we travelled through were frosty. They looked as if someone had sprinkled salt all over them. We all wore four layers of woollens, but we still shivered and our teeth chattered like they were giving ovations to exceptionally good dramas.

I have to say, we were a rather determined group. We walked on and on and on [actually, I don't think I should say 'we', as I didn't walk at all for all that time. I was carried by Martin and James]. Every day, we asked Brown about our location, and he always answered, "We are under the French Alps."

One day, after Martin and I had been woken up due to James stuffing snow in our collars [Will was spared because James was afraid of what the black-haired boy would do to him if he attempted to introduce him to a new day using such a method], Brown announced, "I have a few things to say." We all crowded around him.

I was sitting on my stretcher, which was being carried by James and Martin. Brown began, "First of all, Lewis, I think you stop being carried around." My forehead creased as I looked at him [fine, fine, I admit it. I was getting a bit too used to the good treatment I was receiving].

Brown continued, "Yes, lad, I think that you are now capable of walking on your own feet. You have recovered enough." I nodded, my spirits going down a notch. "And it's a bloody good thing too," James said, looking at me. "You're heavier than a woolly mammoth."

"I am not!" I exclaimed, scandalised.

"All right, all right," Mr. McCartney said hastily before the two of us could begin an argument.

Brown cleared his throat and resumed, "Secondly, Fergusson, I am sorry that I have offended you. Duty comes first." Will exhaled heavily and looked away. Brown rolled his eyes and said, "Thirdly, I would like to inform you all that we are now in Italy."

Chapter 27
A Little Spat

Knowing that we were in Italy raised my spirits tremendously. We were finally out of France and in another country that was much safer to be in [rather, *under*]. I cracked a smile and looked around at the others. Everyone else, except for Will, was looking nothing short of overjoyed.

"Hah! We're finally out of that stupid country where they serve snails and slugs for breakfast!" James yelled, punching the air. "Try not to mention such obscene things, Master McCartney," Martin said, making a disgusted expression. James stuck his tongue out at him and began dancing like some sort of an Egyptian gorilla.

Brown rolled his eyes again. January asked, "Italy is much safer than France, right? So, can we stay above-ground from now on?" "She does have a point, Brown," I said. Brown cleared his throat and replied, "We cannot stay above-ground in Italy because there is a more than major chance that a huge war is going to take place."

I was shocked to hear that. My euphoria burst like a bubble. "B-But..." Mrs. McCartney began. "We cannot avoid it now. Nothing can be done to prevent what is looming over us. Very soon, we shall all most probably be pulled into violence, bloodshed and carnage, whether we like it or not," said Brown.

It only got colder as we continued on our underground way. I began walking with James's support. It hurt a bit at first, but I got used to it after a while. On and on we walked, determined to reach Switzerland. I couldn't wait to get to the snowy nation- it was to be my cocoon of safety for as long as the war would last, after all.

My heel had as good as recovered and my back was doing very well [I pride myself on my self-healing abilities ;)]. I was depending upon my friends lesser and lesser for support. Brown himself told me that I would be as fit as a fiddle very soon.

However, one thing still nagged my mind. The mystery of the dream I had had in which I was a small child of about five still remained unsolved. I really couldn't fathom what that particular one meant.

I thought that I had found out what the 'you must fulfil your destiny' part of the Lord Ares dream meant. I figured that that dream and the one in which I was performing with my Gibson were connected. As much as I hated to admit it, I was rather sure that the dreams were telling me that I was not destined to be a musician and that my future lay in the armed forces. I didn't want to believe what they said to me. 'After all,' I thought. 'Dreams never become reality, right?'

One time, while one of our catch-up-on-your-sleep breaks; I was sitting awake as I was on guard duty. One of our two spirit lamps provided me with light. I assumed that everyone was asleep because we had been walking for quite a lot of distance and everyone was exhausted. I was very tired myself, but I had to stay awake for the sake of our group.

"What're you brooding over?"

I nearly jumped out of my skin when I heard that question. My eyes scanned the scene around me, searching for my questioner. With the help of the illumination the spirit lamp gave, I saw that Will was sitting up, his arms folded across his chest, and looking straight at me with his hazel eyes.

"You're awake, Will?" I whispered. He rolled his eyes and said in an irritated voice, "No, this is my ghost which is talking to you and thinking about just how bloody idiotic you are." He was, as he had been for the past few weeks, in an ugly mood. I decided to not retort.

"Now, why don't you stop looking so pathetic and answer the question I asked you?" He said rudely in a half-whisper.

"Well, I...I was thinking about my dreams."

"What about them?"

"Er..." I looked at Will. His eyes were blazing with the immense fury that had been present within his being ever since his Spencer had been shot.

"Can you even talk, you little buffoon?"

That was enough to raise my temper. I had tolerated enough from William Patrolman Fergusson. "Don't call *me* pathetic! *You* are the one who has been moping around like a loser because Brown served your traitor of a brother right! Brown told you to get over his death, didn't he? Now, wh..."

Will didn't offer me a chance to complete what I was saying. He came straight up to me and fiercely grabbed my collar. Wild anger was depicted on his countenance. "How dare you call Spencer a traitor?" Will asked in a loud voice. I glared right back at him and whispered fiercely, "Be soft!" However, my telling him to do so was of no use. Brown sat up, kicked off the rug he had pulled over himself and hurried over to us. Mr. McCartney stirred in his sleep and so did James. Thankfully, both of them went back to sleep. Brown prised Will's fingers off my collar and looked at the two of us questioningly. "May I have the pleasure of knowing why the two of you were quarrelling?" He questioned, his voice calm but his eyes betraying how vexed he was.

Will mumbled something under his breath. "I apologise, Fergusson, but I didn't quite catch that," said Brown, looking daggers at Will. "Nothing," said Will, looking away. Brown rolled his eyes and looked at me. "What happened?" he asked.

I related everything that had taken place to him. After I finished, Brown said, "Get some sleep, the two of you. Take some rest. Tomorrow is going to be yet another exerting day. I shall take on guard duty."

"Are you sure? Your slot doesn't start until three." I spoke. Brown glared at me intensely and said, "If I wasn't, I wouldn't have volunteered, would I?" His gaze bore through me. I nodded meekly [DON'T make that face! You would have done the same thing had you been in my boots] and went off to my sleeping mat. Will's one was right beside mine. I turned onto my other side so that I wouldn't see his face. The sound of him exhaling heavily as he took his thick comforter around his person reached my ears. Then, for a few seconds, all was silent. Suddenly, I heard the black-haired boy turn over. "Lewis," he whispered. I refused to look at him, thinking that he wanted to hurl insults at me. So, I just grunted. I heard Will take a deep breath in. The next second, he said, "I'm sorry."

Chapter 28

Finally There!

I admit it- I hadn't expected Will to apologise. I realised that I had misunderstood him completely. I had thought that Will would be too proud and conceited to even look at me after our little spat. However, I saw that he had class and that made me feel ashamed of myself. I apologised to him too, but he refused to pay attention to me when I did so. "It wasn't your fault that we started quarrelling in the first place," he said.

After our fight, Will's temper changed for the better considerably. Though he still wasn't as much as a chatterbox and a goof as he was before the 'Spencer Incident', he didn't stay angry the whole time and spoke politely with everyone.

The weather only got colder as we proceeded onwards. Martin went down with a chill and so did Mrs. McCartney. Our air-breaks were horrible- we needed oxygen badly, but it was awfully icy outside.

Brown gave each one of us a small bottle filled with a transparent liquid. I got to know what it was immediately after I smelled it. The fluid was eucalyptus oil. Brown asked all of us to apply it onto our noses and foreheads. I, of course, knew [and still know] that eucalyptus oil was an excellent medicine found in nature for curing colds and chills. We were to use the oil as a preventive measure Brown and Mr. McCartney had together given us a long lecture on 'prevention is better than cure' before Brown handed the bottles out to us. Brown also warned us to keep our warm things on at all times as the risk of getting frostbite was always present.

We continued walking. I was totally exhausted-both mentally and physically. It seemed to me as if our journey would never end. Every minute of our way, I was hopeful, wishing for Brown to tell us that we were finally in Switzerland. However, for what seemed to me like millenniums, he broke no such news to us.

Finally, Brown told us that he had something to announce. My spirits went up several notches as I looked expectantly at him. For the first time in a long, long while, I cracked a smile. However, it slid off my face the minute I took a closer look at our guide's face.

Brown's eyes were poignant. The corners of his mouth had turned slightly downwards. He looked very sad. No, forget sad. He looked *tragic*. Mrs. McCartney was the one who voiced what was most probably running through all of our minds. "What's wrong, Mr. Brown?"

He swallowed and eyeballed all of us. "It has happened," he said, looking downwards. Shock and fear mingled with anger seized me. I knew exactly what Brown was talking about. I just couldn't believe my ears. I knew that everyone had been expecting it to begin, but I had never really thought that it would actually start. Call me stupid. Call me an idiot. I deserve it. I was sure that the others in our group were feeling the same way too, judging by the expressions on their faces.

"B-But," stuttered James. "I-It c-c-can't...wh-what will happen to us?"

Brown looked up and said, "The war has begun. It was only to be expected. We have to be ten thousand times more careful now. I have news from one of the British Intelligence Society members that soldiers have been positioned everywhere. Air raids have begun too. Soon, there will be destruction like no one has ever imagined before. People will die in scores. Europe will be left in shambles!

"As for us, we are still a long way from our destination. We must walk with full determination and perseverance from now on. We *have to* put in everything we have and reach Switzerland. Time is absolutely crucial now. Not a moment must be lost. We must begin moving with our full strength, confidence and energy!"

And we did just that.

On and on we went, never once looking back. We reduced the time we took for rests. I was, of course, feeling highly strained, but I couldn't let my weariness get to me. I had to go on, after all. I had to reach my destination. I had to reach Switzerland.

This went on for God only knows how many weeks. Brown no longer bothered to predict the amount of time that had passed. All he was concerned about was getting us to safety. I was very impressed with him. He was risking everything, including his very life, to ensure that we were fine. In my eyes, he deserved a place in the Isles of the Blest.

Also, once or twice, we heard the sounds of bombs blasting and grenades being dropped. It was awfully frightening. Thankfully, none of us got hurt.

And then, after walking for miles and miles, Brown made the announcement I had been waiting so hopefully for- "We are under Switzerland." Needless to say, I was overjoyed. We boys and January began dancing around and singing in a way that would have made an old granny scream, "Hoodlums! Hoodlums on the street!" We were so loud that the elders had to quieten us down. After all, Hitler was still after our guts.

I couldn't believe that our journey had come to an end. We had been through a lot together. My mind simply couldn't register that, or the fact that I would probably not see the McCartneys or Brown ever again in my life.

Brown walked a few yards ahead and, with some effort, shifted a frosty stone slab that [I recalled much later] had been set into the ceiling of the passage were standing in aside. A small opening stared down at us. Through it, I could see the bright blue sky and a snowy slope.

For a few seconds, everyone was silent. Brown looked at us impatiently and said, "Well, do not you all want to enter Switzerland?" Suddenly, I came to terms with the fact that we were finally safe. With a small yell, I raced towards the opening. However, Will beat me to it. He climbed through it with ease and a cry of joy. I went through after Will.

It was a beautiful feeling. We were finally safe and free from passages and tunnels! I jumped and yelled around with Will, acting like a pre-school brat. James came out next. He grinned around and joined us in our antics. Martin exited the passage after James. He did not play around with us, but stood some distance away and watched his, his eyebrows raised and bemused expression on his face.

January came out next. She smiled around at the magnificent snowy landscape. Her parents followed her out. The last one to exit the passage was Brown. He shut the opening behind him and cleared his throat. We stopped our hullabaloo and looked at him.

"Well," Brown said. "We are now in Switzerland and, not to forget, safe and sound. No one will take any action on us here." We youngsters hooted and cheered and the elders simply smiled. Brown continued, his brown eyes shining and a grin tugging at his lips, "Now, we all shall set off for the train station."

"I hope we don't have to walk up to there," said Martin.

"Oh, no," said Brown. "A van is waiting to take us up to there. At the station, we must part. Martin, Lewis and Will, your train leaves in less than twenty minutes. Mr. McCartney, you and your family's train leaves half an hour after theirs. Now, let me tell you one thing. The station we are going to is a cargo-only train station. The nearest station that serves passengers has been snowed up and the others that are close enough do not have trains at times that suit your convenience. Also, there will be less chance of spies spotting us if we go by them.

"That very thought entered my mind too, Brown," smiled Mr. McCartney.

"Good," Brown spoke. "Now, I really think we should get going. The boys will miss their train if we stand around and chat any longer."

Chapter 29

Our Major Mistake

"OUCH! LEWIS! That was my foot!" Martin yelled as I stepped into Compartment Number 7 on S.C.T [Swiss Cargo Train] AQ-38503. "I'm sorry, Martin. It's just too dark in here," I said as I put my other foot inside. Promptly, I tripped over what was most probably a piece of luggage and fell flat on my face.

"Are you fine, Lewis?" Will asked from outside. "Yes," I replied, picking myself up from the floor of the carriage, only to fall down again [it was marvellous luck]. I heard Will climb in and shifted away to give him room.

"It's horribly dark," said Will after a few moments. "Yo, it is," I agreed. "Does anyone see anything that can be used for illumination?" "If it is dark in the first place, how are we going to see something like that, you twit?" Will hissed.

"This carriage is really stuffy. There's not even a small vent. And who knows, there may be all sorts of rodents here," Martin said. I detected a shudder in his words. I don't really mind rodents. From my childhood, I have always thought them to be harmless.

Just as Martin finished what he said, the train's whistle blew and its wheels began moving. We were off to Geneva. We didn't take our luggage with us as Brown had assured us that it would be properly transported to our destination.

I thought back to our parting at the Gotthard Cargo Train Station...

The three of us shook hands with James and Mr. McCartney and saluted January and Mrs. McCartney. I still have no clue why, but my salute had much more flourish in it. Of course, we piled loads of compliments onto Brown, who smiled modestly. If we don't see you again, you can be sure that it is because we have perished valiantly.

I yawned and stretched as the train came to a complete stop. The journey had taken much longer than I thought it would. We knew that we had reached Geneva as all the cargo trains leaving from the Gotthard Cargo Train Station were direct trains. Brown had told us that in the van.

"Now," said Will. "We'll get out of this stupid carriage as quickly and quietly as possible. We shall sneak around the train so that no one sees us getting down, fine?" "Fine," I replied and Martin said, "Let's go." I heard Will opening the trap slowly. I could see some green grass through the open trap. 'How is there no snow?' I wondered to myself. However, I put the question out of my mind. Snow didn't cover every square inch of the ground, did it?

My ears picked up the sound of Will getting out of the trap. I moved towards it, ready to exit the carriage. Just then, Will gave out a small bellow from outside. Immediately, my heartbeat picked up. Had he been caught?

"What happened?" Martin whispered from right behind me. I shrugged even though I knew that he wouldn't be able to see my action and exited the carriage.

The moment I stepped out of the cargo train, my eyes widened with shock. Everywhere I turned, my eyes met with only destruction. Houses had collapsed. Rubble and bricks were scattered all around. The people that were outside had anxious and frightened looks on their faces. The station was in horrible shape. Half of it had crumbled to the ground. Its board had blackened completely. And, there was not a flake of snow to be seen anywhere.

Martin gasped as he got out of the train, "Where are we?" "Definitely not in Geneva," replied Will before sprinting towards the station, without bothering to hide himself. Martin and I took off after him. Miraculously, no one stopped us [I can't stop thanking my stars for that]. We climbed haphazardly onto a platform and went straight to the nearest ticket-window.

Martin asked, "What is the name of this place?" The man sitting there answered in a French accent, "Why, this is Strasbourg! Could not you guess?" I nearly got a heart failure.

We were in the French city that was in most danger from the war! Strasbourg is damn close to the German border! But how could we? Had we...had we climbed onto the wrong train?

My being froze with dread as my mind went back to Gotthard Cargo Train Station. There was another train between the platform on which Brown and the McCartneys were standing and our train. So, of course, none of them would have seen us boarding the wrong train. Also, I remembered seeing in the schedule that Brown had showed us that the train for Strasbourg left only a minute later than the train to Geneva. Brown had told us many times over to climb into the correct train, or else the consequences would be disastrous. However, we had acted like prize fools and gotten into the train that was going to the very last place on the planet that we wanted to be in.

"A-Are you sure?" I asked. The man replied, "Of course I am. I have been working behind this glass pane for nine whole years." He glanced at his watch and said, "You three boys should be careful. Usually, an air-raid begins at this time. Really, it is astonishing that trains still come and go here."

"Well, then, what do you suggest we do?' Will asked. I could tell from his tone that he was utterly flabbergasted [of course]. The man replied, "There is an underground trench about a kilometre to the right of this station. You can take protection there". "Thanks a lot," Martin said. "Good luck," wished the man. "But what about *you*?" I asked him. "What are *you* going to do?"

He sighed in a melancholy way and mumbled something under his breath. I could catch only two words of what he said: 'Save' and 'Marie'. I was about to ask him what he meant, but I didn't because I felt that I would be invading his personal space if I did.

The three of us ran out of the station and onto the road- or at least, what was left of it. Dust, cement, bricks and chunks of other building materials were strewn on it. Ditches and ridges marred what once must have been a smooth and reliable road.

"Let's just get to that trench thingummy fast," Will said, racing towards where the ticket-collector had told us the trench was. Martin and I took off after him. "I just hope the raid doesn't start before we reach it," said Martin. "Martin!" I yelled crossly. "What have I told you about being positive?"

"What the hell do you mean by *positive*? We're going to die, you blithering fool!" Martin bellowed. The next second, he let out a cry of pain. Will had apparently kicked his rear as hard as he could. "It serves you right, you nincompoop," I said angrily. "Whatever the situation may be, you should never be pessimistic. It not only kills your spirit, but also affects your health."

"Don't dare to..." Will was cut off by a loud roaring sound. Like a prize idiot, I began looking around myself for the source of the sound. It was only after a few seconds that I realised what it was. Planes were approaching Strasbourg. The air-raid was not very far away.

"Come on, run!" Will exclaimed, grabbing my wrist and dragging me along. "Hey, mate, I can run without your help," I said, jerking my wrist out of his grasp. "Just hurry along," Will muttered.

The roaring got louder and louder and our pace got quicker and quicker [I know that I sound like a pre-schooler]. I looked to my left and saw a house that was not as badly demolished as the others. "Can't we just enter that house over there?" I stopped and asked, pointing at it.

Will and Martin stopped too and looked at the structure. "I don't know," Will said. "It may not be safe. There's a chance of us getting crushed inside it once the raid begins." "His words do have value, Will," Martin said. "The raid can begin at any time now and we're still quite a distance away from the trench. Let's face it- there is a huge possibility of us dying that way too."

Just as the words left Martin's mouth, a loud explosion was heard. The three of us whipped around to see that the first grenade had been dropped. The air-raid had begun.

"Let's move!" Will cried, running towards the trench. "Will, wait!" Martin called frantically. The hazel-eyed boy said, "I think we should run to the trench. If we enter that house, we'll have to last out until the whole raid ends. If we just get to it, we can forget our woes." And, before I knew what I was doing, I was tearing down the street behind Will. Martin too followed us.

The sound of a blast was heard for the second time. Another bomb had fallen. Strasbourg was being wrecked by German soldiers.

I increased my speed, my breath coming out in pants. My legs were throbbing with pain and my lungs felt like they were on fire. I kept telling myself to move ahead: It was a matter of life and death, after all. I couldn't afford to be a git about things.

Soon, a third grenade was dropped. This one fell very close to where we were. In fact, the dust that rose into the air due to the explosion settled on my sleeves and in my hair and made me hack several times [now that I look back on it, I must have looked like a grandpa].

"Run, Lewis, run!" Will screamed. We were zipping down the street, trying to avoid the debris on the road. I was exhausted. The trench was just not coming. "It's just a little way off now," said Will. "We'll be there before we know it."

Finally, after a lot of running and five more blasts, we reached the trench. Miraculously, none of us got injured. I heaved a sigh of relief and wiped my brow. We were finally safe.

The opening of the trench was basically a camouflaged trapdoor set into the road [I know, such things make repeated appearances in my tale]. Will bent down and pulled the trapdoor open. I looked over Will's shoulder. Many people, young and old, were huddled together. A young woman who was sitting very close to the door screamed as the three of us tried to squeeze inside. Everyone tried to shift in a little to accommodate us and close the door above. No matter how hard everyone tried it was clear that there was not enough space for all of us. Someone had to remain outside to save the others.

"Darn it!" Will yelled, dropping the lid of the trapdoor back into its original position. Martin suddenly said, "I'll stay up. You two go down and save yourselves." "What the *hell* are you talking about, you idiot?" Will shouted.

"I've lost everyone in any case," said Martin. "I've lost my whole family. Also, for some time, I was a terrible drug addict. You two deserve to live more than I do."

"Stop blabbering nonsense," I said. "What are the people of Leicester going to do without their Duke?" Martin looked down and said, "Please don't call me that. I'm ashamed of myself. I have no right to become a Duke."

"Oh, shut up!" I yelled. "I'm the one who's staying out. My father hates me anyway. He won't miss me. My mother will, but I can't-I won't-let any one of you die."

"But your mother will be terribly grieved, won't she? You should live and take good care of her!" Will roared over the noise of the aircrafts. "If anyone over here should die, it is me!"

"But even *you* have *your* mother to look after! Besides, you haven't even met her yet! The two of you are brilliant people, Will and Martin. I am just an idiot and the reason we are in such a situation. You two, save yourselves." I retorted.

"Lewis, all three of us are the reason we are here. Quit blaming yourself! We all should have checked if we were climbing into the proper train." Will bellowed. "Let's stop all this nonsense! Either all three of us stay up or all three of us go down."

"That's right!" I screamed, banging my fist onto the palm of my left hand.

"Please go inside, the two of you," Martin said softly. Tears had welled up in his blue-grey eyes.

"Not without you, mate."

His face was clammy and sweaty, eyes wide and pleading with us. I could see a small tear threatening to fall off the rim of his right eye. "Please," he gasped. "Please do this for me."

"I've made myself very clear."

Will turned to him angrily and said, "Why don't you stop being such an arse and listen to us? We haven't much time; in fact, we haven't almost any time left. Just listen to us, will you?"

"I won't let you two do anything of the sort."

"Face it, chum. There are two of us and you're only one sodding person who's stupidly trying to be a hero. We can easily beat you in an argument."

Martin looked up at the sky. Planes shot across it, dropping grenades and other explosives as they shot across the cerulean sky.

Will said, "There's no use searching for another shelter now. We don't even know where another one will be. Plus, the raid has begun. If we're going to die anyway, let's do so like men."

Martin finally agreed, "We live together or we die together. Nothing else is acceptable."

I allowed myself a weak smile and spoke, "Now, let's face this bloody thing."

We just stood there, smiles on our faces, eyes shining and arms around each other, waiting for our death - we were sure it would come soon.

Epilogue

Six years. Six hard, long years of fighting. Six years of violence. Six years of war. What had they done to the nation? What had they done to *me*?

As I sat, sweaty and dirty, at the long wooden table in the tent along with my comrades, I racked my brains for the answers to these questions. Yes, I had survived the raid. I wish I hadn't. I wish I hadn't lived to witness the dawn of the next day. Unfortunately, however, I did. Which sane person would like to be alive and awake with their two best friends dead?

The moment I had come to my senses in that British Military Medical Assistance tent, I had known that something was amiss. That was evident from the expressions on the faces of the nurses. I was heavily injured and equally heavily bandaged. Every muscle in my body had hurt. The first words that had escaped my mouth were: "Will, Martin, where are you two?".

The nurses had looked at each other. I had posed my question once again. Then, before I could have done anything to stop her, one of them had pricked my arm with a needle. The world had blurred. Colours had swum around in front of my eyes. The next second, everything had gone black.

When I had regained my consciousness again, I had felt slightly stronger. I had asked my question once again. When the nurses had seen that I was not going to simply forget about Will and Martin, they had told me that they were...not in the world anymore.

This piece of news had shattered me. For several seconds, I had simply stared at the wall in front of my bed, unable to believe what the nurses had told me. The two people that meant the world to me were gone.

I remembered everything that I had done with them. I replayed every second of our underground journey in my mind. I thought about the chair incident in that hotel. I went back to my time with Martin on *Naval Boat 23*. I recalled everything that I had done with Will back in Cornwall Naval Defence Camp. Those golden moments were ones that would never be forgotten.

Will and Martin were like comets. They came, lit up my life and went. They made my life 3x better.

Then, suddenly, fury had replaced my shock. Will and Martin had died because of that stupid air-raid. Who had caused the air-raid? The wicked Germans. Hatred such as which I had never experienced before coursed through my being. This was all the Germans' fault. They had killed my friends. And, they were bloody well going to pay.

It was a split-second decision. I don't know whether it was irrational or not. All I wanted to do at that moment was avenge their deaths. And there was just one way to do that: I had to take on the Germans, to fight them on the battlefield. So, in that moment, I decided what I was going to do. I didn't care if I lost my life. Even if I did, it would be for a noble cause. I decided that I was going to fight for my friends, my mother and my country. I had made peace with myself.

Just as I was musing over all this in my mind, General Smith, the person in charge of our tent, entered. We all stood up and saluted him. He saluted back and gestured to all of us to sit down.

"Well, men," he said in his gruff voice. "I have a piece of news for you all." I looked at him, expecting it to be about how we were short on supplies or about the death or abduction of some soldiers. General Smith cleared his throat and said, "My soldiers, Hitler has committed suicide. The war is over. We have won."

Now, reader, you must be expecting all of us to jump up and whoop and dance around in joy. However, we did nothing of the sort. How could we, when there was no reason whatsoever to celebrate? There had been too much of bloodshed. Too much of carnage. Too much of killing.

However, a part of me was happy- I was finally done avenging Will and Martin. Another part of me was astounded. It couldn't understand how Hitler, who had seemed like the sort of man who would win no matter what, had killed himself.

The others at the table were looking at each other, an amalgam of weariness and astonishment on all their faces. Apparently, they couldn't believe that Hitler had done off with himself either.

General Smith walked closer to our table and clasped his hands together. He said, "Yes, lads, it is true. Hitler has murdered himself. Let us pray, courageous soldiers. Let us pray for all those who have fallen in battle-even those from the opposition-so that they may be granted eternal rest and be treated as the true heroes they were and still are. Let us pray for all those who left behind their families and friends and came to fight for their nation. We have emerged victorious in this terrible war. We stood up, our heads bowed and a silent prayer on our lips.

Lord Ares had definitely blessed us with victory, but was that victory enough to compensate for the thousands of lives that had been lost?

General Smith looked up, his eyes holding a poignant expression, and said, "Dismissed!"

The legs of fifty wooden chairs scraped against the ground as half a hundred young soldiers stood up. We saluted General Smith again and began wallking out of the tent, none of us bothering to wait for him to salute back or bothering to file out properly. The war had ended. The moment I stepped out, I wished I had stayed inside the tent for the rest of my life. It was what those residing in Britain will term as 'a simply lovely evening'. The sky was completely devoid of clouds. The last beams of the setting sun coloured the cerulean pavilion above us a pinkish orange. The eastern sky had already turned dark. Cool breezes blew, complementing the rest of the atmosphere perfectly.

Now, faithful reader, you must be wondering why I did not want to emerge out of my tent. I did not wish to do so because the evening reminded me a bit too much of the magnificent evening I had spent on *Naval Boat 23* with Martin. I had chided him for being pessimistic.

I know that I am acting like a sad cypress, but you must excuse me. Only I truly know what Will and Martin meant-and still mean-to me.

I shoved my hands into the pockets of my army suit and began pacing. A large grassy meadow sprawled before me. Soldiers were meeting up with their families and friends. All of them were grinning widely and chattering animatedly.

Suddenly, I felt a hand on my shoulder. I whipped around. George Everest, a friend who I made during fighting and was four years elder to me, was standing there with a bag that I recognised to be mine in his hand and a smile on his face.

It hit me that I had, like an idiot, forgotten to collect my bag from the lockers. "Thanks a ton, George," I said, taking the bag from him. Inside it was a two-thirds-full bottle of water, protein bars...and the small painting of Lord Ares that Will had given me. Yes, during the raid, it was in my pocket and I had kept it throughout the war. It gave me confidence and encouragement. Also, it brought back many fantabulous memories.

"Hey, mate, are you alright?" I looked up at George. His raised eyebrows and eyes betrayed his inquisitiveness. "Oh, yeah, I'm fine," I replied. "It's just that..." I faltered. I couldn't say anything about Will [or Martin, for that matter].

George put his hand on my shoulder and said, "It's okay. Things will turn out to be just fine. And, by the way, your headgear is still on your coconut."

I quickly took my headgear off and put it inside the bag, which I slung over my shoulder. Wind blew through my hair and onto my cheeks. It felt rather good. "I'm exhausted, man," I said, wiping my brow. "You may be exhausted, pal, but I just find myself in wait of a good bath," grinned George. I nodded my head. My cleanliness level was less than that of a pig.

All of a sudden, George exclaimed, "Oh, I almost forgot!" I cocked an eyebrw and asked, "You almost forgot what?" George, however, was busy rummaging into his bag. Finally, he fished out an enevelope and held it out to me. I took it from him and opened it. Inside the envelope was a stack of photographs.

I just had to crack a smile when I saw them. All the photographs showed an extremely cute boy. I figured that it was George's son, Scott, as the infant portrayed in the pictures looked exactly like my chum, from the soft curls on his head to the freckles on the tip of his nose.

I smiled, handing the photographs back to George.

"I can't wait to see him! I just got these photgraphs the day before yesterday. After all, if my son has inherited my handsome and striking looks, I should certainly spend some time with him," George winked. "Ha, stop gloating," I said, punching him lightly on his arm. George opened his mouth to retort, when...

"PAPPA!!!"

Both of us turned to see a miniature version of George Everest running towards us. George gave a whoop and ran towards Scott. George's wife, Isabella, was right behind Scott. George fell to his knees and hugged his son tightly, as Isabella smiled and kneeled down beside them. I beamed at them, turned on my heel [the war didn't really change me all that much, from the look of things] and walked away, leaving George to have his personal space. I decided to go to the refreshment tent and get myself a glass of lemonade.

The refreshment tent was filled with soldiers stuffing lamb and bacon sandwiches into their mouths and washing them down with pints and gallons of lemonade, orangeade and water. To tell you the truth, the whole scene was obnoxious, but no one really cared at that moment. We had lived on meagre rations for six whole years.

"May I get a glass of lemonade, please?" I asked an attendant. She nodded her head, poured out a glass of fresh-squeezed lemonade and handed it to me. As I was gulping it down, I eyeballed the entire tent. And, I almost choked on my drink when I looked at the far right corner of the room. There, downing what looked like his fifteenth glass of orangeade, was none other than James McCartney!

"Oi, James!" I yelled, waving at him. The McCartney looked up and scanned the whole tent with his eyes, looking for the person who had called him [ME!!!]. "Hey, James McCartney!" I bellowed again. James looked around once again, and his eyes settled on my person. He jumped up and ran straight to me. Before I had the chance to say another word, he literally pounced upon my weary body.

"Lewis, pal!" He roared, shaking me until my teeth chattered. "It's bloody brilliant to see you again!" "Blimey, James," I said. "Control your emotions." James laughed and said, "It's good to see you, man. I heard all about the train exchange. All this time, I thought you were dead." I looked down and said, "I'm definitely not dead." James seemed to sense that the Geneva-Strasbourg topic was a sensitive one and he dropped it. "I can't believe Hitler killed himself, though," he said. "Neither can I," I muttered.

"I mean, suicide is such a cowardly thing to do. You're basically running away from your life when you murder yourself. Those who cannot face their lives and live them bravely are chicken, not to mention sub-zero losers. Hitler never seemed to me to be the type of person who would throw away his life just like that," James said.

"I can't agree with you more. I couldn't believe my ears when General Smith broke the news to us."

"Anyway, our families were released from their shelters yesterday when it became evident that Germany was going to lose the war. Mother's been worried sick about me. Father spent hours trying to console her that I won't get killed. And, by the way," he said, an evil glint coming into his eyes, "January's been worried sick about *you*."

"Me?!"

"Yes, *you*, Lewis." He smirked at me. The two of us stayed silent for a moment or two. I kept staring at the grass at my feet. I looked up after a minute or two to see James staring over my left shoulder. I turned around and almost jumped to the Pearly Gates when I saw who it was. My mother was standing a few yards away, a smile on her beautiful face. I sprinted to her and hugged her as tightly as I could. I was seeing her after six years and I never wanted to let her go.

"Hello, son," she smiled as she stroked my cheek. I noticed that she had to stand up on her toes to reach my cheeks. My height had most probably rocketed up. "You were very brave, Lewis," she said. I smiled modestly. "Thanks, Mum," I said.

She smiled, "We caught the first airplane to here after we were no longer needed to remain in our shelters. We were in Madrid. It was then that I saw who was standing beside her. Emitted Cackling looked just like he had six years back, except that his nose was slightly crooked now. I remembered that I had broken his nose with my suitcase on the day I had left home. I also realised that James must have been staring at him as the two of us looked so much alike.

He had a smile on his face. He extended his hand and said, "Good evening, son. You have made me very proud today." I didn't take his hand. I simply glared at him intensely. I was as tall as him now. He took his hand back. Out of the corner of my eye, I could see that my mother's smile had disappeared from her face.

"I don't want to shake hands with you," I said angrily. "You were the one who said that I am no son of yours! So, there's no need to call me that. Besides, I didn't join the army because I decided to follow your words. I fought the Germans to avenge the deaths of two people- two people dearer to me than *you*!" I spat the last word out. There was a long slence.

So...you're still angry, eh?

My inner voice spoke for the first time in years. The last time it had said anything to me was when I had rescued Martin from Clark's Inn.

'Yes, I am. And I have the right to be furious, just so you know.'

Of course I know that. However, is it wise for you to stay angry at him? Do you know every little thing about your father?

'Yes! I lived with him for sixteen whole years. And, by the way, he's not my father. He himself said so.'

Are you sure about that?

'What do you mean?'

However, it did not speak again. I kicked at a pebble on the grassy ground in frustration. There was another silence. Finally, it was broken by my dear mother. "Lewis, darling, I have to tell you something," she spoke. I looked at her, wondering what she wanted to say to me.

"See, Lewis, it's like this," she said. "Your father, he has been suffering from an intestinal tear ever since his childhood. When he was five years old, a rusted nail pierced his intestine. As a matter of fact, he even developed tetanus in that area, but it was cured. However, that tear has yet not been healed. From time to time, he keeps coughing up blood. That tear will never be made better. He has learnt to survive with it."

And then, I got it. It hadn't been me who I saw in that dream of mine. It had been Edward Candling! I could have kicked, punched, clobbered, smacked and thrashed myself good and proper for not thinking of that before. However, it was still hard to believe.

Candling spoke, "When I was five years old, our family solicitor had come to visit my father. I, like you, was rather mischievous in my childhood. I followed them down secretly and eavesdropped upon their conversation. But then..."

"You sneezed. Your father and your family solicitor heard you and you could make out the sound of footsteps approaching the door. You turned around and ran away, scared. However, you tripped and fell straight onto a nail. That is how you got your tear," I completed.

Mother and Candling were looking at me, astonished. "H-How do you know of all this?" Candling asked. I didn't say anything. Candling shook his head and asked, "No, really, *how* do you know?" "I guessed," I lied. I didn't want to tell him about my dreams at that moment.

"Anyway, your father fought courageously despite being ill, Lewis," Mother said. "And, he expected you to follow in his footsteps, which you have done. However, he became angry when he heard that you had different plans for your future. Also, he used to get-and still gets-very stressed due to his tear. So, he vented his frustration onto you. I know that he was very violent to you and behaved very irrationally, but he did not mean to act that way. I admit, even I was quite annoyed with your father that day."

I remembered the way she had taken him to task and asked him to leave me alone.

"I am very sorry for doing that to you, Lewis," Candling apologised. "It was entirely my fault. I was the one who was shamelessly snooping that day. I was the one who tripped over my own feet that day like a clumsy clod. I was the one who took all my anger out on my one and only son."

There was another silence. This one, however, was broken by yours truly. "I am the one who should apologise," I said. "I hated you like anything. I even broke your nose! But you're a true hero, I can see that."

He smiled and spoke, "You are my son, Lewis. I always loved you and will always love you. You mean the world to me. Let me tell you one thing: You are the best son I could possibly have. Like I said, you have made me very proud. As for my nose, well..." His eyes, that resembled mine so much, were filled with admiration for his only son.

Mother's smile returned to its rightful place on her visage. She looked from her husband to her son and back again. As for the two of us, we grinned at each other and firmly shook hands, like father and son.

THE END